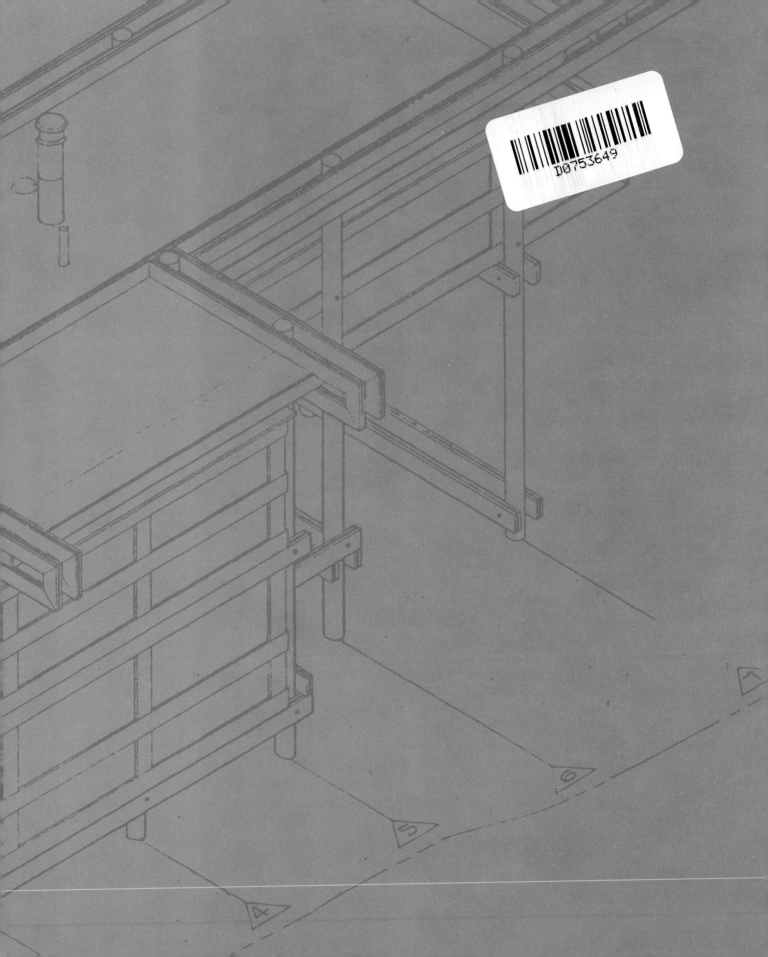

Signature Architects of the San Francisco Bay Area

Signature Architects of the San Francisco Bay Area

DAVE WEINSTEIN

Photography by Linda Svendsen

Gibbs Smith, Publisher
To Enrich and Inspire Humankind

First Edition
10 09 08 07 06 5 4 3 2 1

Published by
Gibbs Smith, Publisher
P.O. Box 667
Layton, Utah 84041

Orders: 1.800.748.5439
www.gibbs-smith.com

Designed by Linda Herman
Printed and bound in Hong Kong

Library of Congress Cataloging-in-Publication Data
Weinstein, Dave.
  Signature architects of the San Francisco Bay area / Dave Weinstein ;
photographs by Linda Svendsen.— 1st ed.
    p. cm.
  ISBN 1-58685-751-7
  1. Architecture—California—San Francisco Bay Area. 2.
Architects—California—San Francisco Bay Area—Biography. I. Svendsen,
Linda. II. Title.

NA735.S35W45 2006
720.9794'6—dc22

2005033527

Contents

Acknowledgments

MOST OF ALL, I NEED TO THANK the hundreds of people who let me visit their homes, and those who let Linda Svendsen take photographs. Often I visited after a knock on the door, and folks invariably apologized for the mess. Not once, however, did I visit a home messier than mine.

Without Gary Goss, who does basic research into local architecture, this book could not have been written. Bradley Wiedmaier shared his in-depth knowledge of architecture and his enthusiasm. Bill Beutner of the Foundation for San Francisco's Architectural Heritage, and Anthony Bruce and Lesley Emmington Jones of Berkeley Architectural Heritage Association provided research assistance and advice.

Waverly Lowell and Carrie McDade of the University of California–Berkeley's, Environmental Design Archives offered encouragement and research help, as did Elizabeth Byrne and her staff at the university's Environmental Design Library.

Foster Goldstrom inspired me to write about Bay Area architects, took me on a tour and provided timely introductions. Lynette Evans, my editor at the *San Francisco Chronicle,* gave me the opportunity to pursue this work.

Architectural historians David Gebhard, John Beach, Sally Woodbridge, Richard Longstreth and Judith Lynch have written wonderful books about California architecture that are invaluable to anyone looking into the subject. David Parry's profiles of Bay Area architects are also an inspiration.

Marty Arbunich provided encouragement and hard-headed advice, as did John Arthur. Russ Levikow, George Espinola, Peter Selz, Gail Lombardi, Ruth Scott, Paul Templeton, Juliana Inman, Steve Staiger of the Palo Alto Historical Association, Ken Duffy, Megan McCaslin, Inge Horton and Craig Hudson went out of their way to help. But most of all, I thank my wife, Mary Barkey, for providing criticism that was particularly useful because she cares about architecture not a whit. ◆

Introduction: Beyond Maybeck

When talk turns to architects who have made their mark in the San Francisco Bay Area, it often stops after two names—Bernard Maybeck and Julia Morgan. Widely admired, they are the stuff of legend. This book takes aim at the little-known Bay Area architects—in other words, everyone else.

People talk about filmmakers with ease, about writers, even painters. But most architects remain unknown. *Metro*, a San Jose weekly, did an amusing story some years back about William Wurster, who's just one rung beneath Maybeck and Morgan on the ladder of architectural fame, but a long rung. It was the rare passerby who could tell the *Metro*'s reporter who Wurster was—and this was on the Cal campus standing in front of Wurster Hall.

Maybeck and Morgan did much to create what we call Bay Area architecture. But they didn't do it alone. The architects profiled in this book were chosen not because they are the best the area has produced, though several are, but because their stories, taken together, provide a solid history of Bay Area architecture—residential architecture in particular.

Many other architects would have made ideal subjects, like the acerbic Willis Polk, easygoing Joseph Esherick, or Bob Anshen, who helped create Joseph Eichler's modern suburban tracts. One day maybe they will.

I started profiling Bay Area architects three years ago, as an outgrowth of articles I had been writing for the *San Francisco Chronicle* about preserving historic buildings. It quickly became apparent that before people realize a building is worth preserving, they need to understand what the building is all about.

What makes a building special? What thoughts, feelings and skill went into its creation? Whose thoughts, feelings and skill?

Maybe, I thought, if people knew more about the architects behind the architecture, they wouldn't have moved so quickly to tear down Vernon de Mars's and Don Hardison's Easter Hill Village, Gardner Dailey's Red Cross Building, or any number of Victorian cottages. Fat chance? Perhaps. But I was encouraged once I started knocking on doors, which was my modus operandi in researching this book.

"Hi, I'm Dave Weinstein," I would say, "and I'm writing about the architect who designed your house." The house could be a multimillion-dollar mansion in Atherton with wrought-iron gates a quarter mile from the front door, or a bungalow in San Jose with an old sofa on the porch. My spiel would be the same. The next thing, more often than not, I would be inside and people who said they only had a few minutes to talk would soon be bragging about their house and its architecture—even if they didn't know the name of the architect.

People who love their houses often attend to them well, and frequently pay attention to the historic style and fabric. And while I didn't see many original kitchens, I did see a few. Residential architecture, after all, is a very special art, among the most intimate.

That's why this book isn't about architecture so much as about houses and their people—the people who live in them, love them, take them for granted occasionally, abuse them, heal them. It's about how houses have fared over time, and how they may fare in the future.

I spoke to many people who have treasured their homes for decades but are sure that once they sell, the home will be demolished and replaced with something grand. They're sad about it, but resigned. I'm also sad, but too optimistic to be resigned.

But let's talk a bit about Maybeck and Morgan. Bernard Maybeck (1862–1957) and Julia Morgan (1872–1957) helped establish how we understand Bay Area architecture, constructing it not only on the ground but in our minds, as something warm and woodsy, unpretentious and, at times, almost invisible, yes, but also sophisticated, witty and willing to take chances.

They knew the Beaux-Arts traditions (both studied at that bastion of academe, the Ecole des Beaux-Arts in Paris) and the traditions that gave birth to the Beaux-Arts—the architecture of Greece and Rome, the Italian Renaissance, Serlio, Inigo Jones and John Soane.

Maybeck and Morgan created brown-shingled houses, Swiss chalets and Classical mansions. Maybeck's Christian Science Church in Berkeley is the favorite building of a large percentage of local architects of every stripe. Morgan gave California its best-designed folly, Hearst Castle. Maybeck inspired the Hillside Club in Berkeley, whose principles of a simple home in natural surroundings helped define the Bay Area tradition.

Maybeck's charismatic personality, Bohemian lifestyle and eccentricities—the last neighborhood he developed required home buyers to build homes with their own hands and tried to ban women from wearing lipstick or smoking—have also proven influential.

But is there such a thing as Bay Area architecture? Many people say no.

Historians have been arguing for years about something called the "Bay Tradition" or "Bay Region Style," that is supposed to characterize at least some of the architects who have called the region home. The term *Bay Region Style* was invented in the late 1940s by a New Yorker, Lewis Mumford, and has been widely disparaged since.

Many people prefer "tradition" to "style," seeing the phenomenon as more one of attitude than of stylistic attributes.

The term refers to several things—the idiosyncrasies of Maybeck; the wit of Ernest Coxhead; the influence of farm houses, barns, and adobes; the influence of Mission Revival; and modern homes that soften the International Style by building in redwood and admitting regional influences like Maybeck and Morgan or touches of Japan.

Few Bay Area homeowners care anything about definitions. They know that the Bay Area is a place like no other and so is its architecture.

Need convincing? Hike through the Berkeley Hills, where houses by Maybeck, Morgan, John Galen Howard, Carr Jones and John Hudson Thomas share vertiginous hillsides and swooping valleys with homes built a generation later by William Wurster, Warren Callister and John Funk, and with even later additions.

The area, with its granite volcanic boulders, decks and roofs built around live oak trees, classically detailed public stairways and forests of redwood and eucalyptus, is a place like no other. The gardens are wild, the domestic adornment unique. It's still inhabited by the same sorts of free souls—professors, musicians, doctors, small business owners—who first moved here when Maybeck was young.

And another good thing about Bay Area architecture is, you probably live in it. ◆

Victorian Finery
Samuel and Joseph Cather Newsom Kept Up to Date

They charm. They beguile. They bamboozle but they don't bully. Victorian houses may be the opposite of everything the Bay Area has come to stand for architecturally. They are neither woodsy, natural, nor unpretentious, nor do they blend with the landscape.

This 1885 Stick Style home by the Newsom Brothers is a San Francisco landmark, adored for its detailed ornament and whimsy, at 1737 Webster Street.

But few houses are as beloved or have become so identified in the public consciousness with Baghdad-by-the-Bay.

San Francisco's Victorians may be brightly painted, plunked onto their sites with little regard to landscaping or landforms, or have their redwood siding made to resemble stone. They are assertive, not reserved; garish, not tasteful.

But when the sun hits them on a late wintry afternoon, it's hard not to fall in love. Locals join fan clubs and preservation societies. Tourists snap their pictures, and no wonder. Victorian homes are entertainers. They're gaudy and pretentious, but in an innocent, ingratiating way. "A gift to the street," architectural historian Judith Lynch called them.

Yet Victorian homes have been widely despised, not only by modernists who dislike their small boxy rooms, or by post–World War II owners or aluminum siding salesmen, who stripped and "remuddled" so many, but by some contemporary Victorian-era architects.

San Francisco architect Willis Polk, whose work was both more historically correct than the standard Queen Anne designers and more modern in its use of space and decoration, called the Western Addition, chockablock with Queen Anne and Stick Style Victorians, "an architectural nightmare conceived in a reign of terror and produced by artistic anarchists."

There were "serious" Victorian-era architects, like Polk and Ernest Coxhead in San Francisco, whose designs were based on rigorous study of historic style adapted and often humorously tweaked to fit modern needs. But the Queen Anne and Stick Style homes that march up and down the city's slopes were something else, the Levittowns of their

Although Victorian houses are often fairly accused of inelegant floor plans and small, isolated rooms, many are surprisingly open and airy. Nick Bell enjoys the open plan of his 1883 working-class Newsom Brothers home in San Francisco, which he has meticulously restored.

WHAT'S A QUEEN ANNE? WHAT'S A STICK?

The Victorian homes that dot the Bay Area are classified today as Italianate (1860s to the '80s), Eastlake or Stick (1870s to the '90s), and Queen Anne (mid-1880s to 1905). The terms were not in use at the time and many houses mix styles. How can you tell one from the other?

Italianates generally have slanted bay windows, fake quoins at the corners to resemble stone blocks and ornate brackets beneath the roof.

Stick Victorians have rectangular bays and decorative wooden slat stick-work, and tend to be ornate. Unlike Queen Annes, however, they do not usually have towers.

Queen Annes may have a gabled roof; more complex massing and multiple roof forms; a mixture of shingled, stuccoed or board siding; and a corner turret topped by a witch's cap. ◆

ABOVE: Even working-class homeowners enjoyed flourishes, including a bracketed door hood. Nick Bell re-created much of the exterior detail on his home, which had been asbestos-shingled when he bought it. **FACING:** A sunburst pediment over an arched living room window adds a touch of the classical to Ed and Marcia Pollack's 1891 Queen Anne cottage designed by Samuel Newsom in San Francisco's Cow Hollow. The gable ends are decorated with heavy vergeboards.

day, the monster homes. It was a nationwide orgy of sawn-wood and lathe-turned balusters and spindles, vergeboards and friezes, bay windows and towers.

San Francisco designers were among the most orgiastic. Chief among these artistic anarchists were brothers Samuel (1852–1908) and Joseph Cather Newsom (1857–1930), who produced some of the city's most attractive Victorian homes. They also designed the Carson House in Eureka, which historian Harold Kirker said "may be the finest surviving example of Victorian architecture in the United States."

The brothers designed about 650 buildings, single- and two-family homes, flats, apartments and hotels, plus commercial and public buildings and churches. These buildings are primarily in Northern and Southern California, with concentrations in San Francisco's Western Addition, Pacific and Presidio Heights, and the Mission Districts.

They worked under the name Newsom Brothers, as individuals, and in partnership with other brothers and with Samuel's sons Sidney and Noble. The Newsoms also pub-

lished pattern books illustrating their designs, and it is impossible to guess how many houses were built elsewhere based on these designs. Some have been spotted in New Zealand and Japan.

Their goal was to sell houses, and they did that by piling on the imagery of the time—medieval corner towers topped with witches' caps, rounded bays, straight bays, angled bays, recessed bays, sunbursts in one gable, fish-scale shingles in

another, classical Palladian windows here, diamond-paned windows there.

Interiors of selected rooms—most often the entry and front parlor, since the aim was to impress—use redwood and fruitwood for wainscoting, fireplace surrounds, decorative balusters, floors and ceiling beams. Stained glass, marble and art tiles, as provided by the client's budget, add to the effect.

Their delight in imagery was playful, but it had its utilitarian side. "We have built Homes for men who were little known until they were occupying their homes," Samuel wrote in 1890, "and then public attention was drawn to them simply because their house was so striking and well carried out."

The Newsoms prided themselves on remaining up to date, so they constantly adopted new styles—Ann Hathaway Style, English Combination Styles, Picturesque Rambling Order Style. As the twentieth century opened and Queen Anne faded, the brothers moved past what we consider Victorian today, building dozens of Mission Revival–style buildings, Spanish Colonials, and Arts and Crafts bungalows.

"Notice the porch," Joseph Cather Newsom wrote in his pattern book *Up To Date Architecture,* about a home he designed for E. P. Marsh in San Francisco. "Isn't it odd? What do you suppose we used here? Why, you couldn't guess. Well, it was Japanese Roofing Tile. Mr. Marsh, being in the Japanese novelty business, came across some of these Quaint Roofing Tiles and we used them here, the effect being very marked, and we were only sorry that more could not be procured to complete the Main Roof."

SAMUEL NEWSOM (1852–1908) and JOSEPH CATHER NEWSOM (1857–1930)

Samuel Newsom.

Style: The Newsoms designed homes and other buildings in various late-nineteenth-century Victorian styles, and then shifted to Craftsman and Period Revival styles to stay current.

Active: The brothers formed a partnership in 1878, split up a decade later, and continued working separately, sometimes together, and with relatives and associates.

Known for: Some of Northern California's grandest Queen Anne homes, as well as more modest dwellings.

Other Victorians: Victorian designers ranged from carpenter-builders who adapted standard plans and bought ornamental woodwork off the shelf, and large building firms like The Real Estate Associates, to sophisticated architects like Henry Geilfuss and W. H. Lillie.

Other Newsoms: The Newsom clan, originally from Canada, produced two generations of Bay Area architects: Brothers John, Thomas, Samuel and Joseph; then Samuel's sons, Sidney and Noble. Archie Newsom shared a last name and collaborated with Sidney and Noble, but was unrelated, according to the family's genealogist, Heather Galanis of Palo Alto. San Francisco mayor Gavin Newsom also belongs to the family. ◆

In their décor, the Newsoms' homes may have been over the top. But the interiors were rationally planned and roomy, and the homes solidly built.

Nick Bell loves his 1883 compact Newsom Brothers home on Waller Street in San Francisco for its easy circulation and ample light. The house was built for a jeweler for $3,250, high for a house of its size. The thirty-five-foot lot is ten feet wider than standard, which allows for a side yard. The Newsoms took advantage of that by placing hallways and stairs in the center of the house to make room for windows. The floor plan downstairs is simple and surprisingly open, with a spacious entry hall and an airy front parlor opening onto a dining room through large pocket doors.

Ed and Marcia Pollack live in one of Samuel's least pretentious homes, a one-story hip-roofed 1,600-square-foot Queen Anne cottage from 1891 in San Francisco's Cow Hollow. Inside, no space is wasted. A short hallway leads immediately to the dining room. To the right, a small parlor blends into the hallway, thanks to a wide door. Behind is a second parlor and two bedrooms. The Pollacks' only complaint with the house is a lack of privacy.

The Newsoms also paid attention to streetscape. Joseph Cather Newsom's plan for "The Country in the City" advised builders "how to arrange a house on a twenty-five-foot lot and have a lawn and garden in front." His plan for "a trio of San Francisco homes" proposed an attractive row of homes, each with different, well-harmonized detailing and with identical rooflines.

Although the Newsoms built some grand homes, including the Carson House for a North Coast lumber baron, their clientele was mainly middle class. They didn't design Nob Hill mansions or the great Peninsula estates.

"They were not boutique architects," says Bill Beutner, a staff member at San Francisco Architectural Heritage. "They weren't architects for the elite."

The brothers were not formally trained in architecture, historian David Gebhard wrote in *Samuel and Joseph Cather Newsom: Victorian Architectural Imagery in California, 1878–1908,* which accompanied a 1979 exhibition. They didn't hobnob with the upper class. "They wished to be in the big leagues," Gebhard said, "But in the end neither really made it."

Samuel and Joseph Cather Newsom, who were born near Montreal and arrived in the Bay Area as children, learned architecture in the office of their older brothers, John and Thomas Newsom, who also designed houses and commercial buildings.

By 1878 Samuel and Joseph were sharing an office in San Francisco and doing well. In 1886 they opened a Los Angeles branch office, headed by Joseph Cather Newsom. Los Angeles was booming. Their work in Southern California included houses designed for merchant builders, large office blocks, mansions for individual clients and

ABOVE, TOP: Joseph Cather Newsom's Whitton House, with its clinker-brick chimney and exposed rafters, is a classic Arts and Crafts bunga-low. ABOVE: A circular window in the front door of the Whitton House. FACING: The fireplace in the Whitton House, a very un-Victorian Arts and Crafts house designed by Joseph Cather Newsom around 1909 to 1912, amuses its owner with its faux supports on the tile fireplace in the dining room.

designs for Piru City, a planned town centered around the developer's medieval castle.

The firm dissolved in 1888, with Joseph Cather Newsom continuing the practice in Southern California. By 1890, after a real estate collapse in Southern California, the Newsoms reunited in San Francisco. They also had an office in Oakland, where Samuel lived. Samuel's son Sidney joined his father in practice in 1893; another son, Noble, joined a few years later.

By all accounts, the Newsoms were methodical work-ers, and lived regular middle-class lives. Joseph seems to have possessed a greater wanderlust than his brother. In 1896 or 1897 he moved to Philadelphia, where he designed homes and churches. It was not common in the 1890s to have Western architects move East. He was soon back home.

Samuel's hobby was studying and photographing

California's missions and other Spanish- and Mexican-era buildings. In a 1907 article in the magazine *Overland*, he claimed to be the first outsider to enter the sacred garden of the monks at the Santa Barbara mission. He also produced a photo story about the early-nineteenth-century Castro adobe in El Cerrito.

Around the turn of the nineteenth century, a new style arrived on the scene that challenged the taste for quasi-historical doodads. Arts and Crafts architects, influenced by such mid-nineteenth-century English theorists and designers as John Ruskin and William Morris, believed that buildings should be honest and informal, use natural materials and unpainted wood, and blend with the landscape. This was more than another "style." It was a new way of thinking, and it was increasingly popular. The Newsoms took to it.

Two Craftsman-style bungalows designed by Joseph Cather Newsom in Berkeley show how adept former Victorians could be with such a supposedly antithetical style. The Newsoms had been moving towards open plans even in

their Victorian cottages. A bungalow in Berkeley's Claremont District carries this even further. From the front door, a visitor looks through a shallow entry hall into a garden room, and then out onto a wide veranda overlooking a creek. A wall of windows provides a modern touch. Upstairs you'll find a newly popular room, the open-air sleeping porch.

Richard Ehrenberger lives a few blocks away in Joseph Cather Newsom's Whitton House, built from 1909 to 1912. When Ehrenberger bought the house in 1962, it was encased in vines. "It looked like a vegetable," he says. With its shingles; massive timber beams; immense clinker-brick chimney; aggressively rustic gables; and several porches, balconies, and garden courtyards, the house still looks like a living thing.

Ehrenberger, an architect and a founder of Berkeley Architectural Heritage Association, loves the home for its vigor, refinement and Oriental sense of proportion.

Craftsman architects bragged about the honest use of materials and structural integrity in their homes. But even Craftsman architects cheated. The dining room fireplace, for example, appears to rest on heavy timbers. "It's faux structure," Ehrenberger says. "It's a little bit silly, a joke in the structure." ◆

NOTABLE NEWSOMS

Among Newsom houses that are readily viewed in San Francisco are the following:

1737 Webster, near Japantown This 1885 home by Samuel and Joseph Cather Newsom has a wildly ornate façade. It was moved to this site to make way for redevelopment.

975 Grove, near Alamo Square An unusual corner turret, decorative brickwork and an emblem with the image of a bear are features of this 1886 house by the two brothers.

The former homes of Isaac Magnin and his two daughters can be seen at **1478 through 1482 Page Street,** near Masonic. Notice the historic plaque.

An attractive pair of Queen Anne homes designed by Samuel in 1889 can be seen at **2602** and **2604 Pacific Avenue.** The house at 2604 was once stuccoed over. The decorative detailing has been re-created.

If you're heading north, the **Carson House** at **143 M Street** in Eureka shouldn't be missed. ◆

A wide, columned doorway opens from the entry hall onto the front parlor in the Pollacks' surprisingly informal home.

RESOURCES FOR VICTORIAN FANS

San Francisco Architectural Heritage owns the Haas-Lilienthal House, a grand Queen Anne home, runs tours and programs, and maintains extensive archives.

2007 Franklin Street
415.441.3000
www.sfheritage.org

The Victorian Alliance of San Francisco holds monthly meetings in Victorian homes in San Francisco and advocates for preservation.

415.824.2666
www.victorianalliance.org

The Frankens' clinker-brick fireplace and stepped stairway rails are Leola Hall signatures. The interior woodwork is fir, not redwood, an economy measure.

On Spec
Leola Hall Made Her Mark with Craftsman Homes in Berkeley

The Craftsman-style house—woodsy, informal, with big fireplaces, cozy nooks, medieval detailing and a prudishly modern concern for utility and "honesty" of materials—bloomed at the turn of the past century.

Based on the nineteenth-century English Arts and Crafts Movement, the style was developed in America by high-end architects such as Greene and Greene in Pasadena, Bernard Maybeck in Berkeley and Frank Lloyd Wright, who built large and rambling, often eccentric homes for individual clients.

Within a few years, the Craftsman aesthetic had trickled down. Speculative builders, many working without architects, began filling neighborhoods nationwide with smaller, simpler versions. These one- and two-story bungalows, sometimes shingled or wood-sided, sometimes stuccoed, sometimes brick, often suggested Cotswold cottages. Today they seem quintessentially American.

In Berkeley, artist and entrepreneur Leola Hall (1881–1930) jumped into speculative building after the 1906 earthquake sent folks scurrying into the East Bay. Hall concentrated in Elmwood, at the edge of Berkeley, which had just started to develop, building dozens of homes that today seem classically Berkeley—brown-shingled, with broad eaves and exposed rafter beams, looking as natural as the live oaks that shaded them.

Hall herself was classically Berkeley, an outspoken activist and suffragist, musician and painter. Her friends included writers, painters and professors. But, as well known as she was for her landscapes, portraits of Edwin Markham and David Starr Jordan, and political activism,

A typical Leola Hall exterior uses brown shingles, rectangular oriel bays, exposed rafters and side-entry doors. This is Jeanne Franken's Berkeley home.

Hall won more fame as a "girl architect."

"I think you're unusual, don't you?" an interviewer for the *San Francisco Call* asked Hall in 1907. "I've known women to try all kinds of men's work, but a girl who selects prospective bargains in real estate, who plans and builds

FACING: Simple, rectangular stepped stairwell rails are a typical Leola Hall touch in the Franken home. ABOVE, LEFT AND RIGHT: Hall loved window niches like this one in her Honeymoon House, with an electric bulb providing illumination both indoors and out.

her own houses and who sells them as quickly as you do, is really unique."

Female architects or builders were rare, despite the presence and fame of Julia Morgan, who was in San Francisco and built homes and other buildings in Berkeley during that time. Hall, who was not a trained architect, sought to produce affordable homes by doing most of the work herself—from buying the lot to designing the house, overseeing the builders and selling the finished product. Hall kept prices low by squeezing two homes onto lots that would normally handle one (her houses are not homes for gardeners), and by standardizing many features.

But the Craftsman worldview—that people flourish best when living amid well-made, artistic homes and furnishings—demanded solid and artful construction. Her houses have held up well, their inhabitants say. Each house had its

WHAT IS AN ARTS AND CRAFTS HOME?

THE ARTS AND CRAFTS MOVEMENT started in mid-nineteenth-century England as a social movement as much as an aesthetic one. Theorist John Ruskin and designer William Morris believed that a return to tasteful, hand-built furnishings, art and architecture, and to a simpler way of life would result in happier well-adjusted people. Gustav Stickley and Elbert Hubbard were among the movement's followers in America.

The movement's impact on society was mild, but on architecture, it was profound. Natural woodwork, exposed ceiling rafters and projecting roof beams, open plans, a return to Gothic and medieval ornament, deformed and blackened clinker bricks, and cozy inglenooks are all marks of the Craftsman home.

There is no Arts and Crafts style. The movement involved various styles, ranging from English Cottage to Mediterranean. California Missions added to the mix in America, as did Frank Lloyd Wright and his Prairie-style compatriots. In Southern California, Charles and Henry Greene pioneered the Craftsman bungalow, which spread nationwide. ◆

LEOLA HALL (1881–1930)

Style: Craftsman. Natural materials, informal plan, low-gabled roof, extended roof rafters. The Bungalow Style is a simpler version based in part on the Craftsman Style.

Active: Hall built homes from 1906 to 1912 or shortly thereafter. Most of her homes are in Berkeley's Elmwood District, with clusters along College Avenue near Ashby Avenue and on Stuart, Piedmont and Pine.

Known for: Characteristic bay windows and side-entry doors, distinctive wooden staircases and wainscoting, clinker-brick fireplaces, economical use of space, and emphasis on large living room/dining room areas.

Other practitioners: Bernard Maybeck and Julia Morgan helped define the Craftsman Style in the Bay Area. Charles and Henry Greene, the Southern California founders of the style, are represented in the Bay Area by the Thorsen House at 2307 Piedmont Avenue, Berkeley, now a fraternity house. Craftsman homes are found throughout the Bay Area. ◆

own touches. One would have five windows in a bay, another four. One bay would be rounded, another squared. Roof and dormer forms varied.

Hall brought much of her personal sense of style to her homes. She may have been a spec builder, but she remained an artist. The *Call* reporter noted her use of the possessive: "I make my doors," Hall said. "I plan my windows."

Hall, described by the interviewer as "trim and serene" with "mild yet shrewd eyes," described her collections—Colonial furniture, spinning wheels, pewter drinking vessels—and confessed that she would have preferred being a musician.

"The least suggestion of formality she was entirely free from," a friend, journalist John D. Barry, wrote in a column after Hall's death. "She assumed that everyone was, not merely worth knowing, but likable."

She also enjoyed social life and getting involved in liberal causes. She headed an effort to block the recall of a Berkeley school official and was vice president of the local Roosevelt Club when Theodore ran for president on the Progressive ticket.

Hall's most famous altercation came when she was driving Chicago suffragist Margaret Haley from one rally to another, her car emblazoned with banners. Arrested for speeding in downtown Oakland, Hall claimed that it was a police setup. "Floodgates of Wrath Are Opened by Arrest," a headline blared. More than 200 women packed the courtroom, and Hall was let go.

She was never a homebody.

Born in San Leandro, Hall came to home building after painting (she studied with Raymond Yelland and William Keith) and designing cushions.

Hall was the daughter of a miner. Her stepfather was a building contractor, and building ran in the family. Hall worked on her first house with a male relative, perhaps her brother-in-law. (Details of her life are sketchy.) Soon she was on her own. Her earliest houses, which include a row on College Avenue south of Ashby, are two-story Neoclassics—Classic Boxes, the style is called—some with Ionic columns, some with her later Craftsman touches.

"According to family lore," says John Malmquist, who lives in a later Hall home on College Avenue with his wife,

The panels behind the breakfront slide open to create a pass-through to the kitchen, one of many handy "women's touches" Franken has detected in her home.

a distant relation of Hall's husband, Herbert Coggins, "she didn't like to cook, but she liked to entertain."

So Hall's kitchens tended to be small—as were her bedrooms. More than in most homes of the period, the space was reserved for the public rooms, for entertaining, political meetings and performances.

The Berkeley Architectural Heritage Association cata-

logued other telltale signs of a Hall home—a front door, often on the side of the house, opening to a wooden staircase framed by tapered Craftsman-style columns; a stair railing that rises as a series of rectangular steps; wooden wainscoting; a rough clinker-brick fireplace, often with seating nooks; wide pocket doors opening to the dining room. Other characteristics include bay windows in the

The Honeymoon House that Hall designed for herself and her new bridegroom contains a grand space ideal for entertaining and for holding political events. At the top of the stairs was the couple's sleeping porch. The joists are redwood, the panels are fir. The exterior of the home, surprisingly enough for Hall, is quiet stucco.

front and miniature three- by four-foot single-window bays for additional light.

Hall often included built-in china cabinets in the dining room, with sliding doors to permit easy access to the kitchen. She is praised by modern homeowners for providing more closets than typical in the period, plus storage beneath stairways. Hall didn't waste space.

Jeanne Franken appreciates her Hall home, which precisely fits the Heritage Association description because of its "women's touches," such as the pass-through from kitchen to dining room and linen closet, and its use of space. "The house has always made sense to me," she says. "A lot of Craftsman homes don't make sense to me."

Franken loves the flow of space and the way the wood glows at night. "I fell in love with this house the minute I walked into it," she says. "I believe in these instant reactions to art and architecture and music. Especially with space. I think space is very emotional."

Large living and dining rooms dominated Hall's houses, nowhere more so than in the 1912 Honeymoon House she built for herself and her bridegroom, an ornithologist and author. "Girl Architect Puts Cupid into Her Plans," one headline read on the occasion of her marriage. Another read "Prominent Suffragette Victim of Cupid's Wiles."

"The house is these two rooms," says Don Feist, its current owner. "Everything else is quite ordinary."

A baronial two-story living room, wood-paneled floor to ceiling, plus a coffered dining room make up the home's public spaces. Feist turns on his stereo to demonstrate the room's fine acoustics. Coggins was a cellist, he explains, and string quartets often performed in the corner.

The upstairs had only a sleeping porch, which the Cogginses used for a rose garden. Downstairs has a kitchen and small master bedroom. The Cogginses never had children, but the Feists had three, turning what had been the sleeping porch into two bedrooms.

Hall's homes are known for their canny lighting, and the Honeymoon House brings in natural light with several

LEOLA HALL HOUSES

Hall's houses are clustered around Ashby and College avenues in the Berkeley Elmwood District. Once you develop an eye for Halls, you'll spot many on College, Stuart, Piedmont and Pine.

The **Honeymoon House** can be seen at **2929 Piedmont Avenue** on Ashby.

A pair of stucco spec houses at **2806** and **2808 Ashby** are alongside the Honeymoon House.

Other Halls include **2800 Kelsey, 2906 Pine, 2848 Russell** and **2624 College.**

Two very early Halls that don't show much of her mature style are **3004** and **3008 College.** The houses at **3042** and **3046 College** show her work in the neoclassic mode. ◆

cantilevered bay windows, triangular miniature bays that house electric fixtures providing light indoors and for the front porch, and high clerestory windows that let Feist luxuriate on the couch while admiring the moon.

The Honeymoon House was one of the last homes Hall built. She and Coggins ran a concrete contracting firm and a small chain of auto parts stores, Patterson Parts. She also painted (including dual portraits of poet Markham, one posed in the morning, when he was surly, the other in the afternoon, when he was voluble).

The couple remained political. Coggins ran unsuccessfully for Congress as "the only La Follette Candidate for Congress." His campaign called for "confiscation of war profits."

Hall, who had heart problems for many years, died at home at age fifty.

She would have found many of the people who live in her homes today to be affable companions. Tom Blackadar and Marcia Johnson, who own a Hall house in the Elmwood District, installed a piano in the living room. Blackadar performs Schubert and appreciates the acoustics. Johnson loves just being in the room. "It's got a real ambience about it," she says. ◆

Coxhead's Churchill House, built in 1892 in Napa, provides a marvelous play of dramatic interior spaces, with the front door hidden beneath a broad stairwell landing. The living room entry landing as well as the dining room and library form one great space.

Strange Talents
Ernest Coxhead's Idiosyncratic Homes Helped Create the Bay Tradition

By all accounts Ernest Coxhead was a proper English gentleman, erudite, reserved, hardworking and meticulous, a bit of a martinet with his children, and a High Anglican to boot. Why then do people describe his architecture as "bewildering," "fairy magic," and "insane," or refer to the architect's "strange talents"?

Few architects have created buildings as quirky, playful and personal as Coxhead (1863–1933), or as historically informed and serious. And few architects cast the same spell.

Anthony Bruce, a Coxhead devotee, remembers the awe he felt as a boy when he visited a Coxhead house with a swooping shingled roof and an abstract arrangement of windows that looked both medieval and modern. "It was the best house I had ever seen," Bruce says. "It was incredible."

Many Coxhead homes resemble Old English cottages, with swayback shingle roofs suggesting thatch. Some look like medieval cityscapes, with varied rooflines and wings that look like individual row houses.

Coxhead slyly mixed seemingly incompatible styles, rustic and refined, in a single building, creating drama on one façade, repose on another and surprise throughout. Roman columns and classical Renaissance porticos, sometimes gargantuan, other times diminutive, appear on otherwise informal façades of natural wood. Rather than working within a historical style, he used elements from different styles to create something new. With their asymmetrically placed windows and doors, and expanses of unbroken walls, Coxhead's homes look very modern.

Coxhead buildings appeal both to connoisseurs and casual passersby, with their sensuous, enveloping shingle

A balcony takes the shape of the staircase within the San Francisco house.

roofs and amusingly incongruous details, like the immense medieval tower of the Churchill House (today the Cedar Gables Inn in Napa), delicately poised on four slender classical columns.

Fans have their favorites. Randy Wilson of San Francisco, a librarian by day, loves the Coxhead house at 400 Clayton Street, built in 1895. "Coxhead makes sophisticated jokes with classical ornamentation that makes post-modernist architects like Robert Venturi, Charles Moore and Robert Stern look like humorless amateurs," he says.

Coxhead's homes are remarkably modern in their use of space. Open the pocket doors to the dining room in the

ABOVE: The heavy entry tower of the Churchill House, today a bed-and-breakfast inn, rests incongruously upon slender classical columns; wings were added later, typical Coxhead conceits.
FACING: Many of Coxhead's homes and churches have suffered visually by replacing shingle or shake roofs, which were designed to appear like thatch. The roof of the Churchill House retains some of its original effects.

Churchill House, built in 1892, and you have a living area as free-flowing as anything sold by Joseph Eichler in the 1950s. "The sophistication of this open plan would seldom be matched until Frank Lloyd Wright's Prairie houses after the turn of the century," scholar Richard Longstreth said. The home won praise at the time it was built as well. "Novelty worthy of imitation," a newspaper observed.

A home from Coxhead's peak period—1888 to 1905—is likely to be dominated by a shingle or shake gable roof that swoops towards the ground past dormers and cross gables. Many of his homes have lost character when shakes were replaced with fire-resistant composition roofing.

Walls of windows are common, and so are walls without windows. "Somewhere on the façade there will be a blank wall," Bruce says. Coxhead loved leaded-glass windows with Gothic curves, and used small oval windows as accents. Interiors are dramatic, with dim low-ceilinged spaces opening into expansive rooms filled with light. Hallways are broad.

Living areas are filled with redwood, including hollow ceiling beams and his signature beveled panels. Classical columns and dentils add formality to mantels and stairwells. Coxhead often used a low stairway landing as a living area. Bruce, who lives in Coxhead's 1906 Van Sant House, uses his landing for the piano.

By 1893 Coxhead had built himself two substantial homes, one in Pacific Heights and another in San Mateo with a view to the Bay. That home, today the Coxhead Inn, is a half-timbered, multi-gabled, fake-thatched affair, with gorgeous woodwork throughout. "When I first walked in here I was dumbfounded," says owner Steve Cabrera, a woodworker himself.

The multi-gabled, shingled Rieber House, built for a Berkeley professor in 1904, looks like a house that has evolved over the centuries. Like many of Coxhead's houses, the rambling 8,000-square-foot home presents different aspects from different sides. "It looks magnificent from the street side," owner Andy Masri says. "Yet in the courtyard, it coddles you."

The roots of Coxhead's style trace back to England, where Arts and Crafts architects were forming a new architecture during Coxhead's youth. Raised in Eastbourne, Sussex, Coxhead studied architecture at the Royal Academy in London, and was influenced by Richard Norman Shaw, an Arts and Crafts pioneer who blended classical and vernacular traditions into a modern style. Coxhead worked with Frederic Chancellor, who restored Gothic churches.

In 1886 Coxhead and his brother Almeric, two years older, moved to Los Angeles to design churches for the Episcopalian Diocese, a denomination allied with England's Anglican Church. Coxhead & Coxhead prospered, eventually designing seventeen churches. Among his notable churches in the Bay Area was St. John the Evangelist in San Francisco, 1890, dubbed "St. Roofus" by the public because of the near-enveloping shingled roof that spilled down from a massive central tower. The church was destroyed in the 1906 earthquake and fire.

Almeric, who had no training, learned drafting in the office and supervised construction. In 1890 the brothers moved to San Francisco. Coxhead joined the Bohemian art scene, befriending the more boisterous Willis Polk, who

ERNEST COXHEAD (1863–1933)

Style: English Vernacular or Cottage style, Arts and Crafts, proto-modern.

Active: Coxhead designed dozens of homes, churches and other buildings in the Bay Area from the late 1880s to the 1920s.

Known for: Shingled, Arts and Crafts–style English vernacular cottages that combine elements from different periods for dramatic effect. ◆

made a name for himself by denouncing the work of older-generation Victorian architects. Polk and Coxhead were both leaders of the Sketch Club and started a magazine to promote forward-thinking architecture.

Polk and Coxhead were soon designing rustic, brown-shingled urban homes, Polk largely on Russian Hill, Coxhead in Pacific Heights and Presidio Heights. Their homes helped create the First Bay Tradition Shingle Style that defines many San Francisco and East Bay neighborhoods.

The homes, with their natural woodwork, attention to the site, large rooms and logical planning, contrasted greatly with typical Victorians, which the younger architects said lacked simplicity, rigor and thought.

In 1898 Almeric joined the Hillside Club in Berkeley, along with Bernard Maybeck, dedicated to creating simple, Arts and Crafts–style homes. That same year Ernest married

COXHEADS TO CATCH

Two Coxhead homes serve as inns:

Coxhead House, 37 E. Santa Inez Avenue, San Mateo, 650.685.1600, www.coxhead.com. This was Coxhead's home.

Cedar Gables Inn, 486 Coombs Street, Napa, 707.224.7969, www.cedargablesinn.com (The Churchill House). A nearly identical Coxhead house in Alameda is owned by Girls, Inc., of the Island City, at **1724 Santa Clara Avenue.**

The Goodman School of Public Policy, Coxhead's old Beta Theta Pi house, was remodeled recently to serve as a school at **2607 Hearst Avenue,** Berkeley.

The 3200 block of Pacific Avenue, San Francisco, is a classic block of shingled homes by Coxhead and contemporaries. Numbers **3232, 3234** and **3255** are by Coxhead.

The **Home Telephone Company** headquarters at **333 Grant,** designed in 1908.

The house at **400 Clayton,** San Francisco, mixes classical with medieval in an idiosyncratic manner.

St. John's Chapel (St. John the Evangelist), at **Mark Thomas Drive at Josselyn Canyon Road,** Monterey, remains an amazing example of Coxhead's idiosyncratic, dollhouse-style churches, although the shingled roof has been replaced.

Another wonderful church is **St. John's Episcopal** at **40 Fifth Street,** Petaluma, and **First Presbyterian** at **112 Bulkley Avenue,** Sausalito. ◆

Helen Browning Hawes, the daughter of an Episcopalian minister and, according to Longstreth, "a favorite belle of the artistic community." Polk was best man.

Helen died a mere seven years later, due to a malady that may have been cancer, says Coxhead's granddaughter Helen Coxhead McFarland, who was named after her grandmother. Coxhead was left with three young children, whom he raised using governesses. The family spent summers at a home he designed in Inverness. Coxhead and his

son Bud sailed Tomales Bay.

Coxhead's career declined after Helen's death. McFarland thinks grief played a part. The 1906 earthquake destroyed some of his finest buildings and may have dispirited him, Longstreth surmised, and suggested that brown-shingled vernacular was falling out of style. New, larger firms were competing for business, and Coxhead was never a strong businessman. Soon Coxhead & Coxhead were only building two or three projects a year, mostly residences.

Longstreth believes Coxhead started playing it safe. "Many of his (later) houses are attractive, commodious and thoughtfully designed, but they lack vitality," he wrote.

In 1910 Coxhead designed the Golden Gate Valley Branch Library in San Francisco, followed by Christ Episcopal Church in Los Altos in 1917. A prominent Mediterranean-style building in Berkeley, originally Garfield School and today the Berkeley Jewish Community Center, it won praise in the professional press in 1915 not for exuberance but for "restraint, decorum, seriousness and austerity."

In 1917 Coxhead worked in war-torn France with the YMCA. After the Armistice, he worked for the War Department teaching architecture to what he called "soldier boy architects." The class toured cathedrals and chateaux, "all in military style, myself in command of the expedition," he wrote to Almeric. The trip was not without its rigors. "We

FACING: Coxhead's Beta Theta Pi House, today a school of public policy at the University of California–Berkeley, was designed to look like a clustered medieval village. ABOVE: A Coxhead house could grow baronial. The Churchill House's wall of windows is typically Coxhead. BELOW: Fine detailing on the newel post of the Churchill House.

sketched until we were frozen stiff," he wrote about the city of Tours, "but the boys felt it was perhaps their last chance before returning to the States, and kept at it."

By the 1920s Coxhead was no longer a central figure in Bay Area architecture. But he was active in professional organizations and an advisor for the new War Memorial in San Francisco. "He is perhaps the prize juror of the profession," *Pacific Coast Architect* wrote, "painstakingly thorough, rigidly honest, excellent judge of technique, quick to recognize talent, originality, organic merit."

His last house, Spanish Colonial outside, woodsy English inside, was built for Bud and his wife in North Berkeley in 1930. Coxhead died three years later in Berkeley after a short illness. The family offered Coxhead's papers to UC–Berkeley. The offer was declined.

Over the years, historians have struggled to define what, if anything, is unique about Bay Area architecture. They talk "woodsy," "natural," "filled with contradictions," "freely borrowing and blending historic elements," "witty." Coxhead supplied much of the wit. ◆

An arched fireplace recalling Louis Sullivan and Frank Lloyd Wright suggests the Prairie-style influence on Luther Turton's 1913 house for Fred Ewer, a prominent Napa farmer and winegrower. Today the 10,000-square-foot house is owned by Beaulieu Vineyards and is used for corporate functions.

It's Tough to Tell a Turton
Luther Turton Left His Mark on Napa in Varied Styles

I f we named our towns after the architects whose buildings define them, the city of Napa would be called Turtonville.

Walking about this historic town, the knowing tourist is besieged by Turton's work. There's the Semorile Building on First Street near Napa Creek, a two-story Italian-style former grocery from 1888 that would look stately if it were less extravagant, with its decorative brickwork and cornice and delicate cast-iron columns. Next door is Turton's ornate Winship Building. A block away on First Street, his Goodman Library looks like a medieval fortress dropped from the sky.

And where First Street turns residential, it's lined for several blocks with Turtons showing off a museum of styles. The turreted Queen Anne–style Noyes-York House and the steep-gabled shingled Francis House are both late Victorian—but how different they are.

The style of the Francis House can also be called "Transitional" because it straddles the extravagant medievalism of the late nineteenth century and the quieter classicism of the early twentieth century. Turton does some straddling himself in the nearby Noyes Mansion, which mixes regal neoclassicism with the country—like Shingle Style.

Turton designed what may be Napa's wildest Victorian—the Migliavacca House (1895), with its domed tower and air of exotica, as well as the radically rustic Craftsman bungalow Olandt Place (1912), hidden away in a rural stretch of the nearby Carneros District, with stone walls and bark-covered redwood veranda posts.

The Goodman Library, home today to the Napa County Historical Society, is one of several downtown Napa landmarks by Turton.

Adding to Turton's stylistic mix are his English Gothic–style Methodist Episcopal Church in Napa and the home he built for himself in the modern, low-slung Prairie Style, created by Frank Lloyd Wright and associates and far

ABOVE: Turton's Migliavacca House, a fabulous Queen Anne from 1895, is a landmark on Napa's Fourth Street. The house was moved to make way for a library.

Style: Turton worked in all the styles of his time—late Victorian Queen Anne, Classical Revival and Craftsman, among others. Some of his best works are Prairie Style, a modern style developed by Frank Lloyd Wright.

Active: Turton worked primarily in the city of Napa and Napa Valley from the 1880s until his death. Most of his work can be found in and around downtown Napa.

Known for: While ranging in style, Turton's homes are known for attention to quality and a feeling of spaciousness. ◆

more common in the flatlands of the Midwest than the coastal hills of California.

So who—and what—is a Turton?

"He did good quality examples of the styles of the day, and he was not afraid to work in the styles of the day," says Juliana Inman, a Napa architect who lives in a Turton home, owns a second, and has restored others. "He was not Frank Lloyd Wright—he was not interested in creating a new style."

"He's one of those good local architects," she says. "Every community has them."

Born in Nebraska, Turton (1862–1925) moved to Napa with his family at age fourteen and spent his entire career there, founding an office in Napa in 1887 after working briefly with a San Francisco firm, McDougall & Son. His buildings are clustered in Napa but can be found throughout the valley and as far away as Yuba City and Woodland. He married and had a daughter.

Turton achieved real success—as judged by the number of commissions, their increasing importance, his institutional clientele (public schools and churches), and his work for Napa's leading merchants, bankers, publishers and winemakers.

Turton's work is not always easy to identify, Inman says. She recognizes Turton touches—his patterns of shingles, his proportions and window sizes—throughout town. But some of the contractors who worked with Turton may have copied identical details in homes built on their own. No matter. Turton is Napa's architect and he is well-loved—even if too little known.

In Berkeley or San Francisco no one's heard of him. In Napa, Inman says, people who live in his houses or attend historic home tours know him. And so do local historians. But even they can be surprised. "He did? I'll be darned!" Cecelia Elkington said when told Turton designed part of the Hatt complex, an old mill that was turned into a complex of shops, restaurants and a hotel.

It takes a lot to surprise Elkington, a volunteer at the Historical Society whose great-uncle built many of the buildings Turton designed. "You're kidding!" she said, when told Turton had also designed Caymus School, a classic one-roomer (since enlarged) near St. Helena.

Prominent Turtons can be spotted all along Highway 29 through the valley, from the Mission-style old Salvador School north of Napa to the awe-inspiring stone Vintage Hall (old St. Helena High) in St. Helena.

One of Turton's grandest homes hides among vines

FIRST FLOOR PLAN

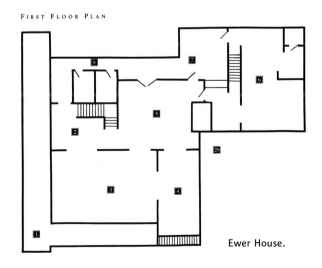

Ewer House.

ABOVE: A broad veranda gives the Prairie-style Ewer House a feeling of ease. Rooms are amply proportioned and stairways are wide.
RIGHT: The Ewer House's broad porch, which extends to a porte cochere, is one of its grandest features.

next to Beaulieu Vineyards in Rutherford. The 1913 Frederich Ewer Mansion (known today as the BV Rutherford House) suggests that the Prairie Style may have been Turton's forte. Nothing could be farther from Victorian than Prairie, an early modern style popular in the Midwest in the 1900s and 1910s that replaced historical caricature and riotous ornamentation with simple horizontals and natural materials that blended with the landscape.

The tile-roofed Ewer House proclaims its affinity with Wright, with its multileveled, strongly horizontal pergola leading to a wide veranda ideal for lazing away the afternoon. Rooms are broad and rambling, providing vistas both inside and out. Beaulieu, which meticulously restored the house after buying it in 1994, uses it for entertaining clients and other functions. It is not open to the public.

Turton's truest fans, of course, live in his homes. They appreciate not only the quality of the architecture, but the connection the homes provide to the valley's past. Inman and her husband's two-story Queen Anne cottage is in a Turton neighborhood. Four of her immediate neighbors are also Turtons, and there are more down the street.

With the pocket doors open, Inman can sit at the piano and see most of the downstairs. "This is not a big room but it feels more spacious because he's borrowed space from the other rooms," she says.

New Orleans expatriate Nina Jacobs, who lives two doors down, immediately became a part of Napa history when she bought her Turton. The woman who sold Jacobs and her late husband the Hackett House, an 1888 Queen Anne cottage, had restored it beautifully, and placed it on the National Register of Historic Places. She also introduced Jacobs to people who remembered it when.

Soon old-timers who had visited the house as children were sharing old photos and stories. "It gave me the feeling of being a real part of Napa," Jacobs says. "Not someone who is going to move in and leave." The photos helped them re-create the house's long-lost finials and roof cresting.

Jacobs had fallen instantly in love with all five rooms and 1,680 square feet of the home, and her affection has grown. She loves the large windows, how the rooms appear bigger than they are, how the detailing continues to beguile. "It is an endlessly fascinating small house," she says.

"When I come in here, I don't turn on the radio or the television or anything. The cats and dogs and I just—are." ◆

TOURING TURTONS

Downtown Turtons include:

The **Goodman Library** at **1219 First Street** (1902). A good first stop for a Turton tour, as it is home to the Napa County Historical Society, 707.224.1739.

Semorile Building at **975 First Street** (1888).

Winship Building at **948 Main Street** (1888). A commercial Italianate structure on the National Register of Historic Places.

The **First United Methodist Church** at **601 Randolph and Fifth** is an English Gothic design from 1916.

Homes in Napa:

First Street residences. West of Jefferson Street, First Street is Turton central. Among his homes that remain private residences are numbers **2109** and **2133**.

The **Beazley House Bed & Breakfast Inn** at **1910 First Street.** This shingle-style home from 1902 is one Turton that can be visited, 707.257.1649.

The **Noyes Mansion** at **1750 First Street,** a brown-shingled neo-classic mansion.

The **Noyes-York House,** a Queen Anne across the street at **1005 Jefferson,** is used for offices (1892).

The **Migliavacca House** at **1475 Fourth Street.** This is Turton's most ornate Victorian; it has been converted to offices (1895).

In St. Helena:

Vintage Hall—Old St. Helena High at **473 Main Street.** Recently renovated, this Romanesque pile of rough-faced stone was built in 1912 and is on the National Register. ◆

FACING: Posts and beams create rhythmic interplay on the Ewer House.
ABOVE: The Kahn-Voorhees House, today the Beazley House Bed and Breakfast,
borrows Colonial Revival detailing and massing.

Herseley-on-the-Hill, a prominent 1903 home in Belvedere, delights with its rich materials and craftsmanship, and startles with its intense play of space. Farr included urns in the piers and banisters.

Designs that Delight
Albert Farr's Witty Homes Went Well Beyond the English Cottage

Before he hit thirty, Albert Farr was designing Tudor mansions in San Francisco that still change hands at record prices, and grand English cottages in Belvedere. The sprawling Benbow Inn near Garberville was his, as was Jack London's tragic Wolf House. Farr designed the defining "downtown" landmarks for Belvedere and Piedmont, exclusive Bay Area towns that scarcely have downtowns, and by the 1920s, he was turning out "some of the largest and most elaborate mansions in Piedmont," says Gail Lombardi of the Piedmont Historical Society.

Farr began by designing rustic but elegant brown-shingled Arts and Crafts houses. He won a reputation for English cottages, created Tudor mansions and Norman farmhouses, and was one of the most successful architects of his time. But by the time he died in 1947 at age seventy-six, Farr was almost forgotten. Newspapers ran perfunctory obituaries, and they defined his work as "Spanish Style."

Even in the 1970s, when architectural historians started resurrecting the reputations of nineteenth- and early-twentieth-century architects, Farr didn't get the credit he deserved. His contemporaries Bernard Maybeck, Ernest Coxhead and Willis Polk won fame for wittily blending historic styles from different periods with modern touches. But Farr was ranked in the second tier, as a talented but mere "eclectic" practitioner. As scholar John Beach put it, Farr was "interested in a 'roses 'round the door' picturesque-ness."

Beach is a founding father of California architectural history, and his judgment carries weight. But Farr's fans don't buy it. "He's an amazing architectural personality who didn't

A Farr mansion in Piedmont suggests a French Renaissance chateau.

miss many beats and had a remarkable ability to stay on top of fashion," says architectural historian Bradley Wiedmaier, who has studied Farr's work. "So much of his work is gorgeous."

Farr worked in many styles, from Tudor in Belvedere to European medieval and Renaissance styles, often in a single building. He designed Period Revival homes—French, Mediterranean, English Cottage, American Colonial, Spanish Colonial, and created a three-quarter-size reproduction of the Tower of Pisa in Chicago. Late in life, some of his homes suggest Streamline Moderne.

What unifies his work is a sense of delight. Farr delighted in details—an angel holding up the entry canopy on one of the "Farr Cottages" from 1898 in Belvedere,

43

ABOVE: Herseley-on-the-Hill established Farr's reputation for English Gothic, with its heavily beamed ceilings and half-timbered effects in living and dining rooms. FACING: Ruins of Jack London's Wolf House.

Palladian windows decorating a medieval entry of a 1908 Berkeley brown-shingle, or urn-shaped balusters that warp like rubber as they follow the contour of the stairs in a 1915 English farmhouse in Piedmont.

"I think it was his pure imagination," says Paul Templeton about the shockingly wide front door of his 1917 Arts and Crafts house in Berkeley. The door's rectangular composition of wood battens and pegs seems both English and Japanese. The house, originally entered through a wooden torii gate, is one of the few that explicitly recalls Farr's boyhood in Japan. "There are all sorts of little subtleties," Templeton says. The stairway piers are finely chamfered, creating a smooth edge that disappears as you slide your hand towards the floor. Templeton does a lot of sliding. "I sort of pet this house like an old dog," he says.

His homes are spatially dynamic. Visitors to Herseley-on-the-Hill, a 1903 home high on Belvedere Island, step into a two-story entry hall, go up a grand handful of stairs into a hallway and stare at San Francisco Bay through a wall of small-paned medieval windows. The dining room to one side and living room to the other are splendid and baronial and form one grand space.

Farr created buildings that tell stories. The Farr Cottages, although a single building of two-story apartments, appear to be an English street of separate homes, thanks to varied set-backs, a rectangular dormer here, a Moorish-arched dormer there. Another Farr home seems like a humble cottage in

ALBERT FARR (1871–1947)

Style: From Arts and Crafts and English Cottage to Tudor, French, American Colonial, Spanish Colonial, even touches of Moderne.

Active: Farr designed houses, churches, public and commercial buildings, mainly in Northern California, from the late 1890s to the early 1940s.

Known for: Belvedere knows Farr for English cottages and Tudor. Piedmont knows him for Mediterranean revival. Fans know him for exquisite and imaginative design. ◆

its lower stories and grows grander above, suggesting a family that has prospered over time.

Sometimes you need to look closely to get the joke. At 2419 Vallejo Street in San Francisco, you might notice that the English Renaissance façade doesn't extend quite the full width of the house—suggesting it was pasted over a medieval townhouse during a sixteenth-century remodel. "He's using the language of tradition in a way that evokes the passage of time," Wiedmaier says.

Farr's life has its own romance and mystery. Little is known today about his habits or personality. He could charm acquaintances. Many of his clients were people who worked in the building where Farr kept his office. Farr enjoyed motoring the countryside and visiting small towns. He was "genuinely modest, so shy of recounting his own achievements," an anonymous writer wrote in the June 1925 issue of

BELOW: The "Farr Cottages" in Belvedere are a bit of old England dropped onto piers over Belvedere Cove. FACING, TOP: Each Farr cottage in Belvedere has its distinguishing touches, including the occasional angel bracket. FACING, BOTTOM: Vertical timbers, asymmetric gables, and windows that pop out unexpectedly are Farr touches in Herseley-on-the-Hill.

Pacific Coast Architect. One of Farr's hobbies was collecting antique furniture, "and it took this interviewer nearly an hour to find out that simple fact."

A sketch accompanying the profile shows a clean-shaven, youthful man with the look of an aesthete in a stiff collar with wind-tossed hair parted in the middle. According to a later interview, Farr smoked incessantly. Friends called him "Bert."

Born in Omaha in 1871, Farr grew up in Yokohama, Japan, where his father helped set up and run the postal system. At age nineteen Farr came to Oakland, where his father served as postmaster. He clearly admired the architecture of Maybeck, Coxhead and Polk, and may have gotten to know them at their sketching club.

Farr apprenticed with a British architect who had offices in Oakland, Frederick Richard Barker, and formed a partnership,

ABOVE: An English manor in Piedmont is an example of Farr's story-telling. FACING: We see a humble peasant cottage abutting the manor house.

Smith and Farr, with Oakland architect and builder Herbert L. Smith, designing an Oakland school in the Romanesque Style, and a tennis club.

In 1893 he was working as a draftsman for San Francisco architect Clinton Day; for the Reid Brothers in 1896; and in 1897 for the design, furnishings and antiques firm Harrold, Belcher & Allen.

By the late 1890s Farr was working for the wealthy clientele and ambitious developers who would support his career for the next half century. A gabled brown-shingled home on Nob Hill won Farr renown, and he was soon "architect of choice in early Belvedere," according to Marty Gordon, chairman of the Belvedere Historic Preservation Committee.

Farr designed a wonderful Arts and Crafts church, complete with a (lost) steeple and fake thatch. Today its nave

serves as City Council chambers. Farr also designed Belvedere's first school (now demolished), and the lively half-timbered offices run by the town's developer, the Belvedere Land Company.

For the company, which was transforming Belvedere Island into a retreat for the wealthy, he also designed the cottages (Bev Bastian, a local historian who lives in one, dubbed them the "Farr Cottages") and the Motor Boat Club House, an imposing structure that Farr himself converted to apartments in the mid-1930s.

Farr, who kept his firm small, lived in a Victorian home he modernized for himself on Union Street in San Francisco, and then in another home he remodeled in Piedmont in 1911, where he lived until his death in 1947. He and his wife, Margaret, had one daughter.

Farr was also something of a father to his nephew, Fred Farr, who won a reputation as an environmentalist in the state senate, helping protect the coast from development. The

A French chateau in Piedmont has wonderful detailing over the doorway and a free arrangement of windows.

senator was proud of his uncle, and attributed some of his interest in the out of doors to his influence, according to Fred's son, Congressman Sam Farr of Carmel.

Tales about Farr as a Bohemian free spirit trace back to his most famous client, Jack London. But there's no evidence that Farr was part of Piedmont's Scenic Avenue artists' scene, which had calmed down by the time Farr moved into a house just down the hill in 1911. He probably knew his neighbors, who included painter Xavier Martinez. Nor is there evidence to suggest that Farr and London were good friends.

Jack and Charmian London hired Farr to design Wolf House in rural Glen Ellen in Sonoma in 1911 after falling in love with another house he had designed. It would have been a 15,000-square-foot bungalow of redwood boards, nine fireplaces, an immense library, and a two-story living room.

Wolf House burned in 1914 as it neared completion. London didn't have enough money to start again or to pay Farr what he owed. "I beg to state that I would appreciate some kind of a payment," Farr beseeched, in a letter in the collection of the Huntington Library in San Marino, California, "as I am very hard pressed for money at the present time."

By the 1920s much of Farr's work was in Piedmont, a wealthy enclave whose look he helped define by designing a master plan for the community center, a park and a ceremonial arch; the Mission-style City Hall and fire house (1909); the town's first school (now gone); and the Piedmont Community Church, with a Baroque interior.

Farr's interest in planning is revealed in the December 1918 issue of *Architect and Engineer* magazine, where Farr contributed "A Plea for Better Business Centers in Our Suburban Towns."

"No one but a madman or one compelled by necessity desires to spend all of his days and the end of them in a great city," he wrote. "To those with sober judgment and with some reward for toil come thoughts of a place in the country not too far from a shopping center and that does not too closely resemble the Babylon from which the departer has fled."

Farr decried the fact that in California, only San Juan Bautista fit the bill, and praised architect Howard Shaw's Lake Forest, Illinois, with its plaza and parking surrounded by two-story retail and residential Tudors that recall Farr's work in Belvedere.

The Piedmont homes that Farr designed with junior partner Joseph Francis Ward included English cottages with rolled shingle roofs, Gothic tracery and tall windows lighting stairways and libraries, Colonials with proper fanlights and transoms, walls of glass facing the garden, crenellated mansions the length of a city block, and French chateaux with swooping garlands.

Farr and Ward continued working into the 1930s and early 1940s, designing a small Colonial home in Oakland, a sumptuous Colonial in Pacific Heights, a shingled ski lodge on the Yuba River, an artist's studio in San Francisco with New Orleans–style tracery on the second-story porch, and a streamlined office for a chemical company. Critic and landscape architect Mark Daniels praised the firm in *Architect and Engineer:* "They are free from the curse of style." ◆

WORTH A VISIT

Downtown Belvedere is a great place for Farr spotting, including the **Belvedere Land Company** at 83 Beach Road, the "**Farr Cottages**" at 80 to 88 Beach Road, the Motor Boat Clubhouse (today apartments) at 30 to 38 Beach Road, and **Belvedere City Hall,** a former church, at 450 San Rafael Avenue.

Downtown Piedmont has **City Hall** at 120 Vista Avenue and the **Piedmont Community Church** at 400 Highland Avenue. Nearby Albert Farr homes include **75 Glen Alpine, 235** and **284 Mountain, 456 Wildwood, 76 Seaview** and **396 Hampton.**

In San Francisco, **2419 Vallejo Street** suggests a Renaissance façade plastered onto an older house; **2350 Pierce Street** is a late Colonial; **9 Presidio Terrace** has a touch of Monterey; **37 Presidio Terrace** is pure elegance.

The ruins of Jack London's **Wolf House** are the centerpiece of **Jack London State Historic Park** at 2400 London Ranch Road, Glen Ellen, jacklondonshp@aol.com.

OR A STAY

There are two inns designed by Farr:

L'Auberge Carmel, 1929, **at Monte Verde and Seventh,** Carmel. This was originally the Sundial Lodge. www.laubergecarmel.com.

The Benbow Inn, Humboldt, at 445 Lake Benbow Drive, Garberville. An English Tudor inn designed by Farr in 1925. ◆

Stucco Style
For John Hudson Thomas, Medieval was Postmodern

John Hudson Thomas (1878–1945) spent his maturity immersed in things English and old, designing homes that appeared half-timbered and thatched. His own English cottage, "Robinswold," with its seemingly hand-hewn beams and hidden niches, occupied a woodsy lot in the East Bay hamlet of Kensington.

When Thomas returned home from a ramble, he would slip up a back flight of stairs to his garret workshop filled with nooks and crannies and decorated with carvings of griffins, where he spent hours creating meticulous renderings in colored pencil of cottages for Atherton or Piedmont, or drawing angels and flowers in designs that suggest medieval manuscripts.

The picture was very different thirty years before, when Thomas made his mark designing some of the most avant-garde houses to startle the East Bay—large stucco houses that are so oddly put together, abstract in form and detail, even shocking, that they still make passersby wonder, "What's that!?"

A classic John Hudson Thomas house looks like nothing else, not like a Mediterranean villa, which it may vaguely recall, or like Frank Lloyd Wright's Prairie Style, which had a major influence, or even like something from the Vienna Secession, the modern movement that was shaking up Central Europe. Thomas's borrowings are obvious, but his buildings—at their best—are entirely his own.

"Thomas's buildings are bizarre and awkward, but they work," says Jim Stetson, a Bay Area architect who discovered Thomas as a student thirty years ago, and then spent months bicycling around the East Bay photographing and visiting them. "His houses have character and life."

Thomas's houses are also among the most noticeable in the East Bay because he built so many of them—at least 160 in the East Bay alone—and many are large and occupy prominent corner lots. Among his houses are two of the most unique in the Bay Area, the 20,000-square-foot, white-columned Viennese-influenced Spring Mansion, and the "Hume Cloister," a medieval cloister complete with gargoyles.

Abstract forms, along with unusual proportions and massing, make Thomas's houses easy to spot. Heavy stucco caps, stucco forms that step down the side of the house, lines that intersect circles, arched windows, and dormers and roof overhangs that intersect in pleasing patterns are all Thomas touches. The beige-colored house from 1913 is at 919 Mendocino Avenue, Berkeley.

The Pratt-Thomas House from 1911, one of a prominent trio at Shattuck and Indian Rock avenues, was Thomas's home for several years. It shows the influence of the Austrian Secession in its abstract forms and details. Thomas signatures include the home's verticality, the use of stucco "buttresses" to suggest strength, grouping two floors of windows, geometric window designs, and arrowhead décor. The globe-topped pillar marks the neighborhood as a prominent corner.

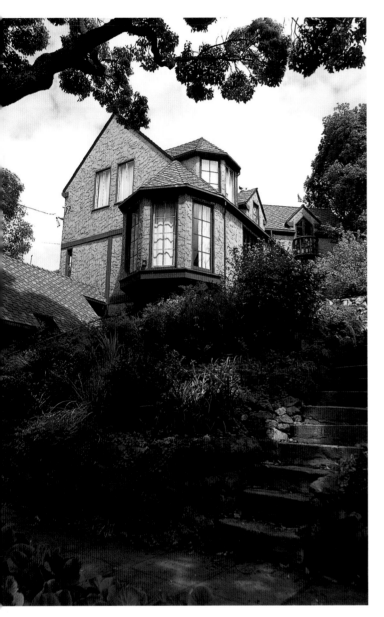

ABOVE: By the 1920s Thomas was designing Period Revival, or even "Storybook" houses, including a complex of four English cottages on Yosemite Avenue, Berkeley, that show such Thomas touches as tall, narrow windows and polygonal bays.

The first two decades of the twentieth century were an exciting period in architecture worldwide, with designers in England, Scotland, Austria and Germany, and America's Midwest moving away from historical revivals to create something new, devising new spatial arrangements, and abandoning applied decoration or creating new forms of decoration that owed little to historical styles. Architects like

Charles Rennie Mackintosh in Scotland, C. F. A. Voysey in England, Adolf Loos and Josef Olbrich in Austria, and Frank Lloyd Wright in Chicago were making their mark.

Even California, backwater that it was, produced men whose work contributed to what later became known as "modern architecture," including Irving Gill and Greene and Greene in Southern California, and Maybeck up north. Thomas is regarded by the historically minded as another proto-modernist, though not as original or consistent as Maybeck.

That is why so many fans dismiss Thomas's later Period Revival work. They feel betrayed. After 1915 or so, historian David Gebhard wrote that Thomas "settled down to two decades of design in the doll house idiom." Foster Goldstrom, one of Thomas's biggest fans in the East Bay, believes his hero simply gave up and stopped fighting for the modern. "I think he gave up being so creative," Goldstrom says. "'They want Spanish-style houses? I'll build them.'"

In fact, this was the second time Thomas dropped one style for another. He began his career in partnership with George Plowman, designing Arts and Crafts brown-shingle cottages, which he dropped for stucco modernism in 1911.

Thomas was no chameleon, however. Homes from all periods share boldness in massing, off-kilter proportions and signature details. His shingled bungalows were never as low-key as promoters of the style, including Berkeley's Charles Keeler, author of *The Simple Home,* would have wished. And his later Period Revival houses never completely dropped his quirkiness.

A Thomas house looks big and bold, even when it's not. Architect Thomas Gordon Smith, who wrote his thesis on the architect, argued that Thomas's clients wanted to "project an image of grandeur and solidity." "If it's small, the house should appear to be large," he wrote. "If it is large, it should appear to be immense."

In Thomas's hands, stucco seems as massive as stone, heavily textured, almost menacing. Louise Hildebrand Klein remembers how Thomas achieved the pebbly texture

Fireplace niches with low arches and built-in seating and shelves are found in many Thomas homes. This niche is in the Pratt-Thomas House.

on the house he designed for her father, Professor Joel Hildebrand. "Dad collected stones from the property. Members of the family took handfuls of the stuff and threw it at the outside walls of the house."

Immense (and fake) stucco buttresses suggest that the home is solid masonry. In fact, Thomas's homes were almost always standard wood frame. Strong, featureless cylindrical piers are another Thomas touch that give weight to his buildings. They are often found at the corners, or between large windows. Thomas also piled on heavy stucco brackets shaped like upside-down steps.

Thomas wasn't the first to build primarily in stucco, which swept into vogue around 1911, but he gloried in its expressive possibilities. Heavy stucco caps loom over doorways and windows. Low arched doorways and windows, often in series, are a trademark. He also loved tall, narrow windows. His houses are rooted in the earth through low stucco fences that seem like extensions of the building. Exterior paving and terraces are as much a part of the architecture as the walls.

But Thomas's houses soar as well. Erupting from the William Locke House, his masterpiece from 1913, is a

JOHN HUDSON THOMAS (1878–1945)

Style: Thomas's mid-period work blended Prairie, Secession and influences from C. F. A. Voysey and Charles Rennie Mackintosh.

Active: Thomas created homes and a few churches and commercial buildings from 1906 to 1945, mostly in the East Bay but also on the Peninsula, Woodland in the Sacramento Valley, Santa Barbara and elsewhere.

Known for: Thomas's homes stand out because of their unique sense of play, proportion and detailing.

Other practitioners: Bernard Maybeck and Louis Christian Mullgardt are other Bay Tradition architects who forged similarly early modern styles. ◆

three-story section that recalls the tower of a Queen Anne mansion. The home itself is a series of masses, one stepping back behind another. Bungalows, it is said, hug the earth, but not one that Plowman and Thomas devised for a hillside on Shattuck Avenue in Berkeley—two stories plus attic over a tall basement, a bungalow skyscraper.

Thomas's fondness for piling mass on top of mass (and, in later years, gable upon gable) didn't always win him friends. "In certain successions of gables," critic and architect Irving Morrow wrote of a 1920 English estate Thomas designed in Los Altos, "the rear ones have a not unjustified air of dissatisfaction with their congested positions."

An abstract play of planes, lines and half-circles is also a Thomas giveaway. Especially in his Viennese phase,

Thomas's sense for geometric décor is as striking as Mondrian's. Flat sections of roof slash into triangular gables, and vertical stucco bands intersect with circular archways over doors. The same geometry extends into the terraces and gardens. Thomas turned his windows into works of art, forming geometric designs with the wood framing that holds panes in place.

Thomas had his own private vocabulary of decorative motifs, particularly the "four squares," a checkerboard design that can be found in the upper corners of his living rooms, atop chimneys, on gateposts, inscribed in patio concrete, and disguised as four clover leafs in stained-glass clerestory windows in a wonderful bungalow on Marin Avenue in Berkeley. Thomas had fun with his squares, which appear in light blue tile, terra-cotta, brick, stucco or glass.

Adding to his repertoire, Thomas created "drip" designs by adding a few falling squares, and decorated his façades with triangular and arrow-head shapes.

Inside, Thomas's homes are simple in plan but dramatic. During his premedieval period, a central entry hall often had the living room to one side, the kitchen to the other, and directly ahead, behind a wall, the dining room. Thomas's spaces were broad, hallways wide, stairways and landings generously proportioned. Landings often included floor-to-ceiling windows.

Thomas stuck his fireplaces off-center, often in large inglenooks complete with built-in seating and bookcases that almost form a room of their own. Fireplace hoods are often beaten copper. Niches are provided for art. Interiors are generally stucco with naturally stained plate rails and broad unadorned baseboards tying together doorway and window tops.

Dorcas and Ted Kowalski fell in love with the Pratt-Thomas House of 1911 when they first saw it. The home is

FACING: The Pratt-Thomas House is remarkably intact inside and out. The dining room has a typical polygonal bay, often found in Thomas living rooms or alcoves as well. Notice the four squares in the upper corners of the windows. ABOVE: A heavy bay atop the entry is another Thomas characteristic. It is said that Thomas installed a drafting table in this window of the Pratt-Thomas House. The low arch is another signature, as is Thomas's four-square motif, which is repeated throughout this house on entry pillars and interior walls.

one of a trio built by developer Pratt near Berkeley's Indian Rock Park, and leased for several years to Thomas. The Kowalskis have preserved everything about the house—including the original kitchen.

Born in Ward, Nevada, Thomas came to the Bay Area with his family as a boy. He had a brother and two sisters. Thomas graduated from Yale in 1902, and from the University of California–Berkeley, in 1905, where he studied architecture with Bernard Maybeck and John Galen Howard.

Thomas worked for two years with Howard, and in 1906 formed a partnership with Plowman, who was ten years older and had also been with Howard. Thomas joined the Hillside

Club, which promoted harmonious development of the Berkeley Hills. Other members
included Bernard Maybeck, Julia Morgan and
Charles Keeler.

It was a propitious time for architects in
the East Bay, where developers like Duncan
McDuffie and John H. Spring were subdivid-
ing the Berkeley Hills, attracting refugees
from the San Francisco earthquake. Thomas
became one of their favorite architects.

After splitting with Plowman, Thomas
had an office across from Duncan McDuffie's
firm, Mason-McDuffie, in Berkeley.
McDuffie sold lots, required buyers to hire
an architect, and made recommendations. A
tour of the Northbrae subdivision, or a
perusal of early photos, reveals that Thomas
was at the top of McDuffie's list.

In early photos of the Berkeley Hills, Thomas houses are
often the only ones to be seen. Many are on corner lots next
to the stone, sphere-topped columns that marked the development as something special. Some of Thomas's homes,
including the Spring Mansion, were illustrated in promotional
brochures for the neighborhood.

FACING: Thomas's own home in Kensington, circa 1928, looks imposing
but is only a single room wide. Thomas indulged his love for multiple
gables. ABOVE: Inside, the home is all nooks and crannies, but french
doors and Gothic windows open it to gardens on every side. Woodwork
appears hand-adzed. The stepped chimney is a motif found in some
Thomas homes throughout his career.

A THOMAS TOUR

Any walk in the hills of North Berkeley will take you past
dozens of Thomas houses. Piedmont is also well populated.
Standouts include:

A home with a wonderfully quirky façade at **919 Mendocino
Avenue,** Berkeley, from 1913.

A classic trio built by developer John Pratt in 1911 at **800
Shattuck Avenue** and **957 through 959 Indian Rock Avenue,**
Berkeley. Thomas lived in 800 Shattuck Avenue.

The house at **1130 Shattuck** has all the Thomas touches, the
four squares, the play of lines and planes.

The structure at **1035 Shattuck** is bungalow as skyscraper, with a

much later Thomas garage below.

Mixing modern and medieval in the details, **1941 through 1947
Yosemite,** Berkeley, is a charming complex of four English cottages.

More gables than you can count adorn this 1939 "cottage" at
1300 Devonshire at Arlington, El Cerrito.

The house at **630 Spruce Street,** Berkeley, from 1941, is part of a
Thomas family complex built for his brother that contains two
hidden cottages below, and once contained a home that is visible
down the hill at **683 Santa Barbara.** ◆

ABOVE: Thomas's garret workshop shows samples of his handiwork, including this carved griffin and his four squares again, this time expressed as four leaves. FACING: A soaring ceiling and Gothic windows provide openness and light in Thomas's home in Kensington.

Besides developers like John H. Spring and William Locke, Thomas's clients included many professors from the university—and several botanists who must have been friends with his father-in-law, Edward James Wickson, journalist, professor of horticulture, a California booster, and author of such best-sellers as *California Fruits and How to Grow Them*. Thomas also designed a complex of homes in Berkeley for his brother Fred, a lawyer, and several other relatives. Also for a family member, he designed a rustic French farmhouse at the foot of Mount Diablo.

Thomas, his wife, Ida Wickson Thomas, and their son John Wickson Thomas (called "Wickson") moved into their Kensington home in 1928. Dick Reimann, who bought the house from Wickson in 1972, gleaned from him that Thomas was an idealist, a romantic, private but not reclusive, and enjoyed strolling to the nearby shopping district on the Arlington.

More can be gleaned from the home itself, which remains unchanged except for a kitchen remodel, and includes the contents of the family library, some of Thomas's drawings and sketches, and his workshop.

Thomas's collection suggests his concerns of the 1920s and 1930s—clippings of English country houses cut from *House Beautiful* and *Pencil Point*; rambling stone and tile homes in Connecticut and Pennsylvania; Charles Greene's stone home in Carmel Highlands; an article on "stucco textures" from a 1922 *Pencil Point* showing a storybook home in New York; books by the Gothicist A. W. Pugin; Gertrude Jekyll's *Gardens for Small Country Houses* from 1912; and *Old Cottages, Farm-Houses and Other Stone Buildings in the Cotswold District* (1905).

The Kensington House is imposing but playful. "You think it's massive, but it's really a skinny thing," Riemann says, pointing out that it's only one-room wide. V-shaped around a courtyard garden, the house has walls of windows, many gables, chamfered beams throughout, and a dining room that's two stories high at one point, and then shrinks to create a cozy fireplace alcove.

"It's the kind of house that can swallow up a lot of people and never feel cramped," Riemann says. "It's a world unto itself. It has that magic garden quality." ◆

The entryway of the Col House opens immediately onto the living room—but not before giving visitors the opportunity to hide their snow-covered boots and mittens, a feature useful on the Great Plains where the Prairie Style was born—but not in San Jose. Leaded-glass windows in the clerestory provide marvelous highlights and swing open to let in air. The well-windowed house is quite a sight at night.

Prairie Homes in Silicon Valley
San Jose's Frank Wolfe Loved to Mix It Up

A century ago Frank Delos Wolfe was the man to see in the South Bay if you wanted something special in a house.

The founder of Del Monte Packing got a shingled mansion in Los Altos Hills topped with three spooky dormers. Businessman Elbert Peck got a stately Classical mansion with a wraparound porch on University Avenue in Palo Alto. *San Francisco Call-Bulletin* editor Fremont Older got Woodhills, a modern estate in Saratoga.

In San Jose, subdivisions created to house the town's merchants and bankers were filled with homes by Wolfe (1863–1926) and his partners, who designed about a quarter of the homes in the Naglee Park neighborhood. Wolfe also designed schools and hospitals, and a cluster of apartments that no visitor to Capitola can forget—the pastel-hued Venetian Court, today a beachfront inn.

"He was without question the most prolific turn-of-the-century architect and one of the most prominent in San Jose," says George Espinola, Wolfe's most fervent fan. "He did more than anyone to define the residential character of San Jose during his era."

But despite designing many local landmarks and having seven buildings on the National Register of Historic Places, Wolfe has been forgotten. Most people who live in Wolfe homes have never heard of him. Most historically minded people know about Wolfe only because Espinola is spreading the word.

And when a San Jose weekly gave Wolfe's astonishing Prairie-style apartment house its "Best Relief from Urban

Classical touches enliven a Wolfe façade in San Jose.

Blight and Redevelopment" award, they attributed the building to a completely different firm that was also named Wolfe and Wolfe.

"San Jose has never been good at tooting its own horn in terms of architectural history," says Espinola, who wrote a book about Wolfe and his first partner, Charles McKenzie.

Wolfe has many fans who had never heard his name, like Pauline Crawford of Los Gatos, who bought one of Wolfe's most distinctive designs, a Prairie home, thirty-five years ago with her husband, Bill. "It drew me," she says. "It was like a magnet. I had to have it."

Wolfe—who designed and sometimes built homes alone, in partnerships with McKenzie, then his son Carl Wolfe, and then with Carl and William E. Higgins—worked in every current style, sometimes in a single building. He was active as a builder and architect from the 1890s to his death. Like many architects of the day, Wolfe was not formally trained in architecture.

"Wolfe's work shows the evolution of the Victorian to modern eras as he worked in the Queen Anne, Colonial, Shingle, Mission, Craftsman, Prairie and Spanish Revival styles," Espinola says. In the Naglee Park subdivision, which got underway in 1902, are many Wolfe & McKenzie Craftsman bungalows, late-Victorian cottages and classical Shingle homes.

Espinola has learned to spot Wolfes. He looks for a large gable roof with projecting dormers, bay windows that "pop out" and are supported by brackets, Ionic columns and shell or geometric designs. Wolfe loved broad porches that penetrated deeply into the house, wide overhanging second stories and covered second-story porches.

His designs are often complex—sometimes willfully so. Some of his designs look wildly creative, others the victim of excessive enthusiasm. Beneath one roofline will be another, like an echo. Gables intersect oddly. A chimney seems to change size and shape as it disappears inside the house, and then reappears above the roof. Decorative details that usually appear at the roofline show up instead below the second story.

"They didn't go by the book," Espinola says. "They threw in a little of this and a little of that. They liked to mix it up."

Rebecca Smith loves her Shingle-style Wolfe & McKenzie home in Naglee Park, with its porch pillars of stone, high-pitched roof and broad porches. The living room is all redwood and wooden beamed, and the fireplace alcove is arched and fills a quarter of the room. "This house feels

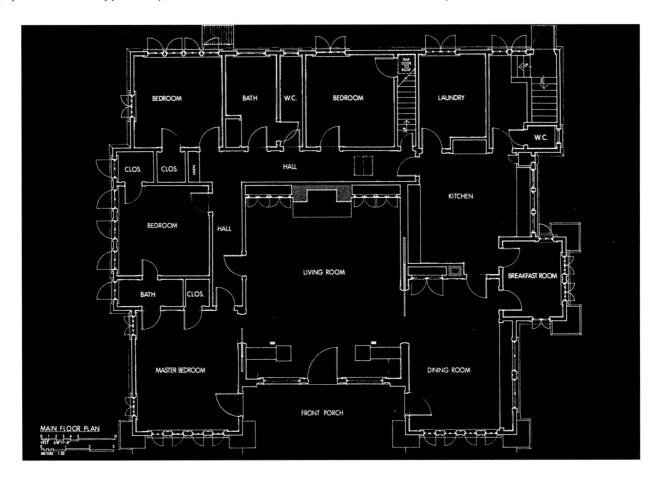

FACING: Wolfe's Col House surrounds a high, light-filled living room featuring clerestory windows, with living and sleeping areas. The house opens through three welcoming doorways onto a large front porch but ignores the backyard, with access only through a service door. ABOVE: The Col House dining room continues the Prairie theme, with art glass in its cupboards.

FRANK DELOS WOLFE (1863–1926)

Style: Wolfe worked in the popular styles of the day—Queen Anne, Craftsman, Neoclassical, Mission and Spanish Revival. Among his most distinctive work were Prairie homes in the style developed in Chicago by Frank Lloyd Wright and contemporaries.

Active: Wolfe, alone or in partnership, designed up to 400 buildings from the 1890s to 1926. Most were houses and most of his work was in San Jose and nearby towns.

Known for: Wolfe's homes show an idiosyncratic mix of details from different styles and a courageous, occasionally foolhardy arrangement of windows, chimneys, rooflines and gables. He loved deep porches and wide overhangs as well as projecting bay windows.

Other practitioners: John Hudson Thomas in Berkeley built some Prairie homes along with an assortment in other styles. Other Prairie homes are scattered throughout the area, including the shores of Oakland's Lake Merritt. ◆

like it's a house that's meant to be shared," she says.

Wolfe is most noted, however, for his Prairie homes, a modern style developed in Chicago early in the century by Frank Lloyd Wright, George Elmslie and Walter Burley Griffin, among others. With their low profiles, bands of windows and simple geometry, Prairie homes still look shockingly abstract.

"It must have driven this neighborhood crazy when they built it," Crawford says of her Los Gatos home, which is surrounded by Victorians and Craftsman bungalows. Crawford's home is odd even for a Prairie home. Shell-like urns hold up the porch, the columns have old-fashioned classic designs in stucco, and the front includes a bay window that looks like it belongs on another house.

"People think it's a Frank Lloyd Wright house," she says. "I say 'yes, my Frank Lloyd Wright knockoff.'"

Prairie homes are common in parts of the Midwest but less so in the Bay Area. San Jose is a hotbed, and Wolfe and Wolfe built about eighty of them, Espinola says. His Prairie phase lasted from 1912 to 1915. "If you see a Prairie building in San Jose, it's probably a Wolfe," Espinola says, "although McKenzie did some on his own."

Wolfe's best-known Prairie home, the Col House, was built in 1913 in the upscale San Jose subdivision of Hanchett Park. Its long, low lines, bands of stained-glass windows and drip-like decorative patterns attract fans. "At night it's like a jewel box," says Victoria Thomas, who lives there with her husband, Marc Morris.

"People know the house," she says, "But not many know the history of the house."

Not everyone is impressed, however. "The best local example of what happens when a minor talent meets a major movement," the authors of *The Guide to Architecture in San Francisco and Northern California* wrote. Thomas and Morris love the house. They lived nearby, and the day after the For Sale sign appeared, Thomas followed. "We're going to buy your house," she told the owner. "Don't worry."

FACING: Original lighting fixtures in the Col House. ABOVE: The Col House is a San Jose landmark on a prominent corner, with its abstract play of flat rooflines.

Rooms are spacious, relaxed and filled with light. The living room entry is a story and a half high and decorated with stained-glass clerestory windows. Similar windows are found in cabinets, the breakfront and elsewhere. In case you miss the Midwest, Wolfe provided built-in containers for galoshes in two alcoves by the front door.

Thomas loves the home despite its quirks. "We had a nice house before," she says. "But once we moved here we just started entertaining all the time. People loved being here. We noticed that at the end of the night people just didn't want to go home."

Thomas and Morris first heard of Frank Wolfe from their real estate agent when they bought the house. Crawford heard of him when Espinola visited.

BUILDINGS BY WOLFE

First Street just north of **Santa Clara Avenue** in San Jose has many Wolfe houses that are now offices, including numbers **444** and **475**.

An interesting Prairie-style apartment house can be spotted at **99 E. Julian Street**, San Jose.

The structure at **45 E. Julian** at Second Street, San Jose, now offices, shows Wolfe's characteristic use of projecting windows.

The Realty Building, at **19 N. Second Street**, San Jose, with unusual floral décor, was designed by Wolfe and housed his practice.

A second version of the Prairie-style Col House at **2662 Monterey Road**, San Jose, today serves as a store, the **Paver Depot**.

The **Griffin House** is on the campus of Foothill College, **12345 S. El Monte Avenue**, Los Altos Hills.

Woodhills, the 1913 Fremont Older House, can be seen from outside on the Fremont Older Open Space Preserve, Prospect Road, Cupertino.

The Venetian Court Hotel is a beachside motel at **1500 Wharf Road**, Capitola. It was designed in 1924 by Wolfe and Higgins. ◆

A native of Green Springs, Ohio, and from a long line of carpenters, Wolfe arrived in San Jose in 1888 and was soon working as a builder with his father, and then in his various partnerships. He worked with veteran architect Joseph O. McKee, Espinola says, where he met coworker Charles McKenzie.

Wolfe may have taken over McKee's practice when he retired. As his career advanced, Wolfe was always the senior partner, Espinola says.

Besides building custom homes, apartments and small commercial buildings, he says, Wolfe built some homes on spec early in his career—and lived in one while building the next. His wife, Nellie, would do interiors and the garden. Wolfe had a dozen addresses in ten years.

Wolfe liked to motor and had one of the first cars in San Jose, it is said. He had a fishing shack in Moss Landing and a weekend house in Capitola. Wolfe died of cancer in 1926. Carl, who continued as the "Wolfe" in Wolfe & Higgins, died five years later.

Espinola, a Sunnyvale architect, grew interested in Wolfe in 1990 because of a love for the Prairie Style. He found a 1907 "Book of Designs" by Wolfe & McKenzie showing ninety-six homes—without addresses. He was soon driving the South Bay looking for them, and poring through old

FACING AND ABOVE: Wolfe's houses ranged from late Victorian neoclassical to imaginative Arts and Crafts classic boxes to abstract Prairie-like designs to quirky bungalows.

magazines and other records. He's found eighty of the homes.

He's located Wolfe buildings in Sacramento, Santa Maria, Napa and Berkeley. Espinola suspects many remain to be discovered.

Espinola hopes that knowing about Wolfe will help preserve his work. The Willard Griffin House, for example, built for the owner of Del Monte, has been decaying on the campus of Foothill College for many years and eventually may be torn down—even though Ernest Kump, the architect of the modern campus, based his much-admired design in part on elements of the house, including the dual-pitched roof. Espinola was part of the Committee to Save

the Griffin House, which tried to rescue the home in the mid-1990s. They raised enough money to repair the roof but not to rehab the entire structure. The home is on the National Register of Historic Places. But the home is structurally unsound and may not be salvageable, according to a representative of the college.

Espinola is encouraged that more people are becoming aware of Wolfe. "Now you're starting to see in the real estate ads, 'Oh! Wolfe & Higgins!' or 'Classic Wolfe & McKenzie, Naglee Park,'" he says. "So yeah, the tide is starting to turn." ◆

Broad beams and low arches evoke old Spain in this 1930 Monterey revival house owned by Liz Simon and Mark Heising. Doorways swing open to the outside.

California Colonial

Birge Clark Mixed Romance with Realism in Palo Alto

For much of his career, architect Birge Clark's stock-in-trade was romance. His faux-adobe homes splashed with hand-painted tile, wrought-iron lanterns and sunny courtyards evoke images of mantilla-wrapped senoritas. But Clark (1893–1989) was no romantic. He enjoyed "Early California" style, as he called it, but he prided himself most on how well his designs worked.

In Palo Alto they worked just fine, giving the architecturally eclectic city much of its Spanish flavor. Known as Palo Alto's first architect (when he opened his office in 1922 he was one of only two licensed architects between San Francisco and San Jose), Clark remains its favorite. He is responsible for more than 450 buildings in town, including many downtown landmarks.

Neighborhoods are packed with his homes, and brokers brag when they have one for sale. Clark, an outgoing man with a sense of humor, was active in community affairs, and many people remember him fondly. The city once held a Birge Clark Day, and fans just call him "Birge."

"You go to Redwood City, you go to Menlo Park," Palo Alto Historical Association's historian Steve Staiger says, "people never heard of him. But in Palo Alto, he's our Maybeck, he's our Julia Morgan."

But how well do people really know him?

Clark is best known for "Spanish Eclectic"—like his famous Norris Home (created in the 1920s for authors Charles and Kathleen Norris), the Lucie Stern complex from 1932 and the Ramona Street commercial district, with its picturesque courtyards and wrought-iron grilles.

Clark and his clients loved picturesque detail, including tile risers and flooring as well as wrought-iron lighting fixtures and banisters. These are from the Heising and Simon House.

But Clark's work ranges farther—to modern ranch-style homes, Streamline Moderne and commercial glass boxes. His Spanish style dominated his work of the 1920s and '30s, and aspects of it can be found throughout his later work. But even during the height of the Period Revival craze, of the '20s and '30s, Clark didn't stick to Spain.

"In that block from Webster to Cowper," Clark wrote about Coleridge Street, "there is this English Elizabethan style . . . next to it is a two-story tile-roofed residence showing Italian influence with a Palladian motif for the front door. . . . Next to that a large Monterey Colonial with a balcony all the way across the front . . . and on the corner what was called at the time 'Early California.' This is the only block in Palo Alto in which I designed every house."

So what exactly is a Clark? Did Clark simply adopt Spanish Style because it was a craze? Did he add anything to the style? Why did he drop it—or did he really drop it?

There are those who think Clark didn't care much about "style" at all; that he was more interested in how a building worked, and that David Clark—his brother and, from 1928 until he died in 1944, partner—was the impetus behind the wrought iron and tile. Architect John Northway, who worked in Clark's firm in the '70s and was a student of Clark's at Stanford, says Clark's main focus was the technical side of architecture, although he appreciated aesthetics.

Clark's son Malcolm says his father appreciated how well Spanish Style worked. "He felt it was attractive and functional—particularly in this climate."

ABOVE: Art-tile risers add charm to the Heising and Simon House.
RIGHT: The second-story balcony marks the Monterey Colonial Style, which blended New England with California adobe.

ABOVE: Clark had dropped explicit Spanish motifs by 1947, when he designed this Palo Alto home owned by Elspeth Farmer and family.

Clark defined the style, which he called "California Colonial," "Early California" or "Mission Revival," as providing an "enclosed feeling"; homes were built around a patio, with thick walls, tile roofs (sometimes shakes or shingles), the liberal use of iron or plaster grilles, verandas, a deeply recessed front door and lots of arches.

The homes looked like adobes, presented blank faces to the street with small windows, were generally L-shaped and had large glass doors opening onto a patio that served as an outdoor living room. Clark studied how the old adobes were built and how they functioned. His son Dean remembers his father saying of the style: "It just seems to flow together."

Spanish Style soared in the 1920s. Santa Barbara adopted it as a design theme. Statewide, missions were being restored. Zorro was a popular character in a novel and on the screen. The style appeared in Florida and the Southwest—and in places like New Jersey and Maryland that had never seen Spanish soldiers or a presidio.

"By the middle 1920s this California Colonial Style was breaking out all over the state and I happily espoused it," Clark wrote. It was, he said, "a basically indigenous style" and well-suited to California life. Clark clearly enjoyed the design of indoor-outdoor living embodied in the casual indoor-outdoor way of life that is embodied in the architectural style. He was an athlete and outdoorsman—he took wagon trips as a child with his family to Yosemite, honeymooned in the High Sierras, camped and hiked into his eighties, and celebrated his ninetieth birthday by riding every roller coaster at Great America. On his ninety-sixth birthday Clark rode in a hot-air balloon. An adventurer to the end, he died in Egypt. The day before he died, he achieved a lifetime dream—visiting the Pyramids.

The orientation around an interior courtyard also appealed to Clark's affection for family. Never a workaholic, he spent much time with his wife, Lucille, and four sons. Clark, who was proud to have spent his life in Palo Alto, referred to the town as an extended family.

Clark's family was prominent in town. His father, Arthur B. Clark, arrived in town in 1892 and headed the Stanford art department. Birge celebrated his sixth birthday in Paris, where his father was studying with Whistler. Clark's sister Esther won renown on the Peninsula as a pediatrician.

A. B. Clark also designed a number of homes on campus, including a Stanford landmark, the Lou Henry Hoover House for Herbert Hoover and his wife. The starkly simple house, built in 1919, seems a bit Spanish and more than a bit modern, much like the stripped-down proto-modern quasi-Spanish homes Irving Gill was designing in Southern California. Birge Clark worked on the building with his father.

The Clarks were friends with the Herbert Hoovers. Clark's parents baby-sat the Hoover children. Clark was at Hoover's home the night he was elected president and the night he was defeated four years later.

Clark did his undergraduate work at Stanford (and later taught there for twenty-two years) and got his architectural degree from Columbia University in 1917. He commanded a balloon observation company during World War I and won the Silver Star after being shot and parachuting to safety.

From the mid-1920s on, he prospered with Spanish or "Early California" houses. His brother David joined the firm in 1933. In 1946 Clark formed the firm Clark and Stromquist with Walter Stromquist, and took on a few more partners as the years went by.

During and after World War II, his firm did industrial and hospital work for Kaiser Permanente in a style that was decidedly modern. After the war, Clark designed

BIRGE M. CLARK (1893–1989)

Style: Known for Spanish Eclectic, "California Colonial"— "Call it whatever you will," Clark said.

Active: 1920–1970s, mostly in Palo Alto.

Other practitioners: Bertram Goodhue in Southern California and George Washington Smith in Santa Barbara pioneered Spanish Colonial Revival. Variants can be found throughout the Bay Area in any mid-1920s to mid-1930s neighborhood. ◆

many public schools and did work for Hewlett Packard. He designed few houses after the 1950s. But it is his residences, along with his community buildings, that are best remembered today.

The Monterey Colonial that Liz Simons and husband Mark Heising share with their children shows Clark at his picturesque best, with its characteristic balconies and veranda along the entire front, polychrome tiles in the entryway and on stair risers, hand-hewn ceiling beams, a sunken living room with floor-to-ceiling glass doors, and a dominating fireplace. The walls are adobe-thick—Clark accomplished this by doubling up the wooden framing, providing the requisite mood—and keep things cool on even the hottest days, Heising says.

The **500 block of Ramona Street,** a Spanish-style historic district. Clark designed most of it. Artist Pedro de Lemos designed the buildings with the more exotic touches, including courtyards with serpentine stairs.

The **Police and Fire Building** at **440 Bryant Street,** a senior center today, is a Spanish Colonial from 1927.

The **President Hotel** at **488 University Avenue,** from 1929, is apartments today.

The **Post Office** at **380 Hamilton Street.** It has a tile-roofed arcade and ornate lobby.

The **Lucie Stern Community Center,** from 1935, at **Middlefield Road and Melville Avenue,** blends Spanish and Moderne.

The **Hoover House** is atop **Cabrillo Avenue** on the Stanford campus. Its primary designer was Clark's father, A. B. Clark.

Other Clark homes can be found throughout town, with one concentration on the **400 and 500 blocks of Coleridge Street—455, 470, 502, 526, 544** and **570.** Landmarks include the Stern houses, **1950, 1960** and **1990 Cowper Street;** a lovely Monterey Revival at **512 Coleridge Street;** the **Casa Abierta,** for novelist Kathleen Norris, at **1247 Cowper,** and the Dunker residence at **420 Maple.** ◆

Down the street, Megan McCaslin lives in the house Clark built for his own family in 1936. Historians call it Streamline Moderne for its curves or Early California Ranch for its low-slung profile and relative lack of Spanish trinkets. But McCaslin has added Turkish runners, a crucifix on the wall and a tiled fountain in the yard. The stucco house retains some wrought iron and tiles, and the L-shaped plan resembles Clark's more "traditional" ranches by extending the roof rafters to cover the patio and providing unimpeded access to the courtyard. All of this suggests how Spanish Eclectic served as a forerunner to the more modern ranch style—and even later styles that emphasize clean lines and outdoor-indoor living.

An even more modern Clark is the 1947 ranch-style home of Elspeth Farmer, who calls it "Birge Clark meets Frank Lloyd Wright." Out front, the façade of skinny Arizona flagstone looks more mid-century Modern than Hacienda. Inside are wide-open spaces designed for a family that loved to entertain and dance. Wrought-iron grilles and art tile cannot be found.

But out back are the same Spanish Style rafters extending over the patio. "It focuses completely on the yard," Farmer says of the home. Step onto the upstairs veranda, with its terra-cotta floor and unbroken plaster walls, and gaze into the patio below. You can almost hear the castanets. ◆

The living area and hallway open to the garden in the Farmer House. The home's plan is as open as his Spanish courtyard homes and retains the same easygoing feel.

Taking Whimsy Seriously
Carr Jones Created Medieval Cottages that are Surprisingly Modern

The style is called Storybook, Fairy Tale, Disneyland or Hansel and Gretel, and the adjective most often applied to it is "whimsical." In Hollywood, where the style developed, its earliest exponents were motion picture set designers—experts in faux everything. But Carr Jones, one of the great Storybook builders of the Bay Area, took his work very seriously. Both his architecture, and people who know him, suggest that Jones (1885–1965) was faux nothing. "He was his houses," says Lana Kacsmaryk, Jones's daughter-in-law.

"He was just pragmatic and practical," says Ruth Scott, who lives in Mill Valley in the last home Jones designed. Jones was no stage designer, she says, but was rooted in the nineteenth-century Arts and Crafts tradition with its emphasis on honest craftsmanship and natural materials. "I call my house a peasant house," she says.

Scott wrote a book about Jones, and argues that "storybook" or "fairytale" are the wrong words to describe his architecture. "They're non-destructible, livable houses," she says. "Fairytale to me means cutesy, gingerbread."

Jones homes may have turrets and spiral staircases, arched doorways and swooping rooflines. But they are also fire resistant, she says, and filled with modern touches like radiant floor heating (his first use of radiant heat was in 1936 in a house in Walnut Grove) and walls of windows. He also pioneered the kitchen island, which is found in several of his homes.

Unlike some Storybook builders, whose fairytale features were add-ons to standard plans, Jones crafted his

FACING: Ted Montgomery installed an organ beneath a true Carr Jones signature—a half-timbered wall of glass, not altogether Elizabethan—in his 1931 Piedmont home. The massive beams, apparently hand-hewn and minuscule in scale, are also Jones touches.
ABOVE: A fireplace bellies out from the dining room wall and the brickwork seems alive in Montgomery's dining room.

CARR JONES (1885–1965)

Style: Storybook, Fairy Tale, Hansel and Gretel. Jones developed an idiosyncratic version of this already-idiosyncratic style based in the Arts and Crafts tradition. He used brick and other natural and recycled materials to craft homes that recall peasant farmhouses blended with California missions.

Active: Jones built from 1914 to the early '60s, primarily throughout the East Bay.

Known for: Fine brickwork, swooping roofs, turrets and arched doorways, balconies, and glass-filled gable windows.

Other practitioners: William R. Yelland created Normandy Village on Spruce Street near the UC–Berkeley campus and other Storybook monuments. Normandy Gardens on Picardy Drive in Oakland is a superb example of a Storybook subdivision by architect Walter Dixon. ◆

homes the way a medieval craftsman would have, often living on-site along with his craftsmen and working alongside them.

Jones studied engineering, not architecture. He did his own designs and contracting and much of the handiwork. His work indicates how much personality and seriousness a builder could bring to a style, even one as seemingly hokey as "Storybook."

Storybook homes differ from their more sedate Period Revival cousins by striving even further to evoke medieval or rural Europe. Instead of relatively restrained Cotswold cottages or Mediterranean villas, we have homes that evoke the Brothers Grimm.

On a typical Jones house you'll see brick outside and in, curves and random patterns. Roofs sway as though weighed down by thatch, and shingles splash across like waves. Homes are often L- or U-shaped, and the ends of the wings often curve. One wing of the house often faces the courtyard with a California Mission–type arcade.

It may be well constructed of brick, but Montgomery's house sways like centuries-old wattle and daub.

ABOVE AND LOWER RIGHT: Arched doorways, iron hinges and latches, and art-tile doorbells are other Jones effects found in Montgomery's house. FACING: A narrow, vaulted hallway leading to the dining room and kitchen poses dangers for tall visitors in Ted Montgomery's house.

Inside you will find a two-story living room with an immense fireplace and a spiral staircase leading to a balcony; floors of randomly arranged terra-cotta and tile; and built-in, hand-carved cabinetry. Walls are thick—sixteen inches or more—and often curved.

Jones never left California, friends say. He got his ideas from *National Geographic* and *Architectural Digest*.

Many of his materials were scrounged. Used bricks were plentiful and cheap after the 1906 earthquake, and he used recycled timbers and phone poles, refrigerator tubing for radiant heat, and disassembled old stoves to create built-in kitchen islands.

One sure Jones touch is a pyramid-shaped gable end filled with glass and decorated with curved beams—like half-timbering with glass between the timbers instead of mud mixed with thatch. The effect is medieval, modern and startling, and brings in a lot of light.

Ted Montgomery enjoys the view he gets from the Chippendale armchair near the fireplace—through a curving corridor and several arched doorways to the dining room

beyond. He also loves surprising Jones fans—they often ring the bell and ask to look—by taking them around back to an 800-square-foot mother-in-law cottage Jones added to the property in 1954. It's got bracketed doors, a medieval chandelier, a wall of glass facing a canyon, and a low-pitched shed roof. It's vintage mid-century Modern. "He wasn't as traditional as you think," Montgomery says.

Another surprisingly modern Jones house was built in Pleasant Hill in 1948, a rambling ranch with curved brick walls and a sod roof. It was demolished in 1996.

No one knows how many structures Jones built. Twenty-seven buildings built or substantially remodeled by Jones can be readily documented. There are undoubtedly more. At least twenty-four are extant. Almost all are houses.

At least five are in Berkeley, six in Oakland, three in Piedmont (counting the mother-in-law cottage), six in Contra Costa County (at least one demolished), three in Marin, one in Palo Alto, and one in Rancho Cucamonga in the Southern California desert. Some, like the restaurant Postino in Lafayette, have become local landmarks.

Jones himself never made much of a mark as a Bay Area personage. He never craved fame, Scott says. "He was a content man within himself." Nor did he seek wealth. "He was a working man and he was not in it for financial reasons," she says. He never sought jobs. Clients came to him after seeing one of his houses.

Friends describe him as a mild, soft-spoken man who listened more than talked. When he talked, Scott says, "it was about architecture and how you did things."

Jones was a strong man of average build, but very short, as are his doors. Jones loved to invent—he developed a form of adobe that could withstand rain without being plastered, Scott says—and he loved building. But he wasn't ambitious, she says.

"Somebody said to me, 'Carr Jones would never have worked a day in his life if he didn't have to eat,'" she says. But he was an elegant man with fine manners, Kacsmaryk says, and attentive to the details of daily living. "You wouldn't set a milk carton on his table," she says.

Jones, who was born in Watsonville and raised in Monterey, moved with his family to Berkeley and received a degree in mechanical engineering from UC–Berkeley in 1911. After college he spent several years living in the Yosemite area and working in lumber camps.

Some accounts say he studied with Maybeck. Scott says it isn't so, but he undoubtedly knew the great Arts and Crafts–style architect. Two of Jones's earliest buildings are in the Berkeley hills north of campus where Maybeck lived and did much of his building.

The homes, built in 1914 and 1916 before the Storybook Style took hold, are Craftsman in tone along the lines of Maybeck, mixing wooden board-and-batten siding with brown shingles, and are complete with Swiss chalet balconies. Another early home is the Hippard Ranch, built in 1916 in Rancho Cucamonga. The home was green before its time, with a cistern to save rainwater, wisteria-shaded pergolas and heat vents to keep things cool, and an "Egyptian" cooling pond in the center of the U-shaped patio.

By the mid-1920s Jones was building in his mature style.

One Carr Jones owner in the Berkeley hills describes how his home was built, with information gleaned from neighbors who watched: Jones and his wife and a crew of six or seven workers moved onto the site, built a brick wall, and then started on the house. Five years later it was done. Jones also turned a flatbed truck into a mobile home for himself, complete with a ladder leading to a sleeping porch on its roof, Scott says.

Jones's most ambitious plan never came to pass, an entire neighborhood of eleven homes he hoped to build on a square block north of Berryman Street, between Shattuck and Walnut in North Berkeley. The neighborhood, called Holly Tree Park, was planned with Edward Bolles, the architect of record.

Jones, who was twice married and raised a stepson, built a sod-roofed home for himself and family in Orinda in 1948. In 1954, Scott says, he was "discovered" by Mrs. Fulton of Fulton Shipyards in Antioch. Jones found himself remodeling many buildings at the shipyard and at her home, and living in a home she owned not far away—and remodeling that. He worked for Fulton until he died.

By the 1960s Jones was suffering from severe arthritis. He was ill when Ruth Scott and her husband, Alan, sought his services in 1964. They knew his work because Alan Scott's aunt lived in a Jones house in Walnut Grove.

"He liked us because we wanted to do the work ourselves," Ruth says. Jones visited the site, a hillside in Mill Valley, and drew up a plan. The work was done by the Scotts and their children, a small crew, and by Doug Allinger, Jones's stepson.

A home Jones built for his brother in Palo Alto casts its spell from behind a flowering field. The home is built around an interior courtyard.

Jones died in October 1965, the day they started work, Scott says.

Though Allinger, a mason, had absorbed Jones's style and ethos, he had never worked with him. The Scotts' home was his first Carr Jones–style building. He has since built several, including some that are well known in Contra Costa County, and he continues to work in the Carr Jones tradition.

Living in a Carr Jones home has challenges as well as charms—though Montgomery, a tall man, says, "In the years I've lived here I've only knocked my head once."

Most people who live in his homes stay there awhile and care for them, Scott says. "People do get possessed with Carr Jones houses." ◆

Easy, Elegant and Up to Date
Gardner Dailey Brought Modern Architecture to the Bay Area

Seen from the street, there's nothing outrageous about the Berliner House, just a pair of redwood boxes and a quiet wall of glass. But in 1938 when it appeared in San Francisco's sedate Jordan Park, the home raised a ruckus.

"One time I heard a screech of brakes," says Gabie Berliner, who was a child when her father built the house. "A car had stopped in the middle of the street. They came and looked in the windows, mouths agape, eyes wide, like it was something from Mars."

It was an odd reception for a Gardner Dailey home. Something of a boy wonder, he had been designing immense Spanish and English Cottage mansions on the Peninsula, and neoclassic townhouses in Presidio Heights for a decade and a half. But in 1935 he switched to modernism and never looked back.

Along with William Wurster, who was the same age and whose career followed the same stylistic arc, Dailey (1895–1967) introduced modern architecture to Northern California. They were "the two leaders of the time," says San Francisco architect Craig Hudson, a student of their work, who says Dailey's buildings were just a bit more polished and refined than Wurster's.

A line of freestanding piers in the entry gallery adds to the feeling of lightness and drama in the Bowman House in Kentfield. The home is elegant, provides broad spaces and a formal dining room, opens everywhere to gardens and terraces, and has a curved staircase that suggests Streamline Moderne.

Dailey remains an important figure, not just because he helped create the folksy Bay Region style of modernism, influencing hundreds of architects who followed in the 1950s, but because his homes possess charm, warmth and fine proportions that set them apart from the competition.

A Dailey home has an easygoing air, as though it's settled onto the site and let out its belt. There are extra-wide hallways, doors and windows, and windows are unusually tall. Sliding-glass and screen doors slide away to turn "rooms" into gardens. Although Dailey's dining rooms seem formal, his plans call them "garden rooms," and many are surrounded on three sides by glass and gardens.

Dailey began as a landscape designer, and on most of his homes collaborated with Thomas Church, a pioneering modern landscape architect. "It was so smooth, to watch those guys work together," says Russ Levikow, an associate architect with Dailey in the 1950s and '60s. "Both were big talents yet could work together so well."

Dailey loved his details, clean metal or white wood window trim, door pulls with Streamline Moderne "speed lines," and simple flush molding. "He was a bearcat about that," Levikow says.

Broad curving staircases add elegance, with cylindrical metal banisters that could have come from an ocean liner. Blond-tinted or natural wood paneling brings warmth to otherwise cool interiors. Dailey's homes are rarely confrontational. Todd Blake, who restored Dailey's 1937 Ets-Hokin House in Ross, calls his style "non-angry modernism, if you will."

In a typical home from Dailey's modern period—it commenced in 1935—"you go in and you go right out again," Levikow says. Across from the entry you'll find a garden, a terrace, or a hallway that opens completely to the outdoors with the slide of pocket doors.

"It's so easy to open the house up," Charles McBurney says of the 1938 home he shares on a Marin hillside with his wife, photo-realist painter Linda Bacon. The Bowman Home was designed to maximize views of Mount Tamalpais with walls of windows and glass doors that open onto terraces.

The home, creamy white and sophisticated with a sunken living room and originally with maid's quarters, is indebted to the chaste International Style but with sensuous Streamline curves.

Dailey would on occasion play up these Art Deco-ish curves, as in a wonderfully ship-like home in Woodside with a curved prow and an upstairs deck that suggests the bridge of a ship. More strictly modern in appearance are some of his urban homes, including a wood-and-glass box in Sausalito from 1939 that, some people believe, was largely the work of Joseph Esherick, the most famous graduate of Dailey's atelier.

Dailey's mature homes also included rambling woodsy structures that, from curb-side, can look more standard 1950s ranch than "modern." Bill and Jackie Gomez's long (120 feet) and low home in Woodside, a shake-roofed, gabled affair from 1939 with the typical Dailey walls of glass onto the garden and a garden-style dining room, is as unpretentious as Dailey gets. An exterior of clear-heart redwood planking finished only with linseed oil gives the home a barn-like look. Inside it's a rustic forest lodge, with a terra-cotta-tiled hallway beneath exposed fir rafters.

After visiting the laid-back Gomez home, it's shocking to drive by Dailey's traditional mansions from a few years earlier, medieval mansions with diamond-pane windows, wrought-iron lamps, and cornice brackets shaped like angels. For one 1934 Storybook mansion in Woodside, Dailey provided a matching dog house by the front door.

But look closely and you'll see similarities. One immense English "cottage" in Woodside is L-shaped around a wonderful old oak, like so many of Dailey's modern landscapes. Church also worked on many of these earlier homes. When it was originally built, the home had an outdoor dining area scooped out of the living-dining wing. Many of Dailey's "traditional" mansions had immense walls of windows, though they may have been diamond paned instead of metal trimmed. Many of their interiors were as warm and woodsy as his later work, albeit with medieval crossbeams instead of flush redwood paneling.

It's not clear why Dailey made the switch from traditional to modern—or why in 1935 he decided that he could do so. It didn't hurt his career, which started out strong and never flagged.

Levikow, who continued Dailey's office with two partners after his death, flips through a list of projects as he sits at Dailey's old worktable. "The names in here, it sounds like the social register in San Francisco," he says. They include De Bretteville, Bechtel, Theriot, Fleishhacker, Ghirardelli, Haas, and in Modesto, Ernest Gallo. Levikow still occupies Dailey's original office near Union Square.

Dailey himself didn't come from money. Born in St. Paul, Minnesota, Dailey moved to San Francisco as a teenager.

During World War I, he won a Purple Heart as an Army Air Corps pilot. On a reconnaissance mission north of Verdun, Dailey flew low through searchlights and anti-aircraft fire, took a hit, and was forced to land. His injuries left him blind in the right eye. "Through skillful piloting," Dailey's commander reported, in a successful effort to secure the flyer a Distinguished Service Cross, "he managed to land his machine in darkness without injuring his observer, although he himself was suffering severe cuts about the face and eyes, which rendered one eye permanently useless." Dailey remained a captain in the air reserve for another ten years.

After the war, he graduated from Stanford, studied engineering and drafting at Healds Business School, and

The elegant Bowman House on a hillside in Marin County reveals touches of Streamline Moderne in the curving staircase. Linda Bacon's paintings add a personal touch.

worked as a nurseryman. He never got a degree in architecture. He spent a year in Mexico doing engineering for
a development company.

Details of his early career are scarce. He worked for Julia
Morgan, designing terra-cotta décor for an Oakland store,
and serving as chief gardener at Hearst Castle in the early
1920s until running afoul of William Randolph Hearst.
"Dailey," Hearst cabled Morgan, "do we not need."

And Levikow knows Dailey worked for Morgan's contemporary Willis Polk because Dailey would pass on tips
he'd learned from the pioneer.

Another story Levikow heard: Dailey was working as a
landscape architect and the client said, "I like you. Do the
house too."

Dailey got his architect license in 1927, opened his office
and within a year was designing a country estate for the
prominent speculator Julian Thorne in Woodside. Dailey
was thirty-two. Levikow believes Dailey's outgoing personality
lead to his quick success, along with an advantageous marriage to Marjorie Dunne, daughter of a well-connected
San Francisco lawyer. They married in Paris in 1926.

"Gardner was a noisy, garrulous Irishman at heart,"

FACING AND ABOVE: This house, owned by Charles McBurney and Linda Bacon, opens to a series of terraces and gardens, and the dining room is as formal a room as Dailey ever created in his modern period.

The brick fireplace surround—one brick wide—is typical of Dailey's work, as is the warm woodwork in the Price House.

Esherick recalled in an oral history for the Regional Oral History Office at Bancroft Library in Berkeley. "He was very funny, incredibly funny." Dailey would describe a room as "like being inside a ballerina's skirt," and tell hilarious stories of his days selling garbanzo beans in Mexico.

During World War II he spent time in Brazil on the war material effort as chief architect and engineer for a rubber company.

Dailey loved the arts, especially Goya and the Impressionists, collected Asian art, and served on the board of the San Francisco Museum of Art (later Museum of Modern Art) for more than twenty years. He traveled widely, collected exotic plants, and was president of the Strybing Arboretum Society, where you can still sit on the Gardner A. Dailey Bench.

"Yet at the same time," *Fortnight: The Magazine of*

California reported in December 1946, "he often looks and acts like one of the hard-faced, two-fisted bosses and bricklayers who use his blueprints."

Dailey, a natty dresser, drove a Mercedes and a Lincoln, and lived in an apartment high on Nob Hill, a "redwood box" he designed for himself in Carmel, and later a weekend home in Saratoga, Levikow says. Dailey moved in high-society circles. When Finnish architect Aalvar Aalto visited San Francisco after the war, it was Dailey who threw the party. Probably the only project Dailey did after 1935 that wasn't modern was for a friend—the tiki bar interior of Trader Vic's.

Dailey served on San Francisco's Planning Commission for four years, including a stint as president. In 1962 he helped organize a group to preserve Chinatown's "priceless architectural heritage from the ravages of helter-skelter development."

Dailey, who never had children, divorced his first wife and remarried. His second wife served as the firm's "house mother" when Levikow worked there.

As a boss, Levikow says, Dailey was affable, "but he could turn it off too. He didn't like people who were pretentious or pushy. He called them 'name drippers,' not droppers."

Unlike Wurster, whose firm became a regional powerhouse, Dailey stayed relatively small, with never more than three associates. By the 1960s, when Gardner A. Dailey Associates was doing the master plan for UC–Davis, buildings for UC–Berkeley, Stanford and BART, hotels in Hawaii, and a World War II Memorial in the Philippines, the firm had about seventy employees.

Levikow says the firm never got bigger than Gardner wanted. "I'd say to him, 'Gardner, that guy wants to build a $3 million house.' 'Well, he's not going to do it here,' said Dailey. 'That guy's going to be a pain in the ass.'"

"He always said we ran a 'limited practice.' It meant he did work with the people he wanted to work with."

In 1966 Dailey underwent brain surgery for an ailment he never discussed. "For a year he did OK, then he slowly seemed to drift away," Levikow says, sitting at Dailey's old

BAY AREA TRADITIONS—FIRST, SECOND AND THIRD

NOT ONLY DOES THE BAY AREA claim to have its own regional tradition of architecture, it has three phases of the tradition, according to a widely accepted taxonomy devised by historian David Gebhard.

First Bay Region Tradition (1880s–1920s) The work of Maybeck and Morgan, Willis Polk, Ernest Coxhead, and a slew of designers of brown-shingle cottages. First Tradition homes can be shingled and rustic Arts and Crafts bungalows, or sophisticated shingled or stucco townhomes by Ernest Coxhead or John Hudson Thomas. Simplicity is one characteristic and playful allusions to historical precedent are another.

Second Bay Tradition (1920s–1960s) Modern architecture took hold slowly in the Bay Area, and slyly as well. William Wurster moved from grand Period Revival mansions to simple but expensive farm-style houses in the late 1920s. Gardner Dailey, John Dinwiddie, and others began building low-slung modern homes of redwood in the 1930s. What followed was a regional modernism softer than the International Style that was spreading from Europe to the United States.

Second Tradition homes, which include Eichlers, often used redwood and plywood, and consciously borrowed from Maybeck, vernacular traditions and Japan.

Third Bay Tradition (1960s–today) Charles Moore, Joseph Esherick and members of their firms helped develop a more vertical but still woodsy architecture most easily seen at Sea Ranch, overlooking the Pacific in northern Sonoma County.

Third Tradition homes are often boxy and oddly shaped, with single-slope shed roofs that lack eaves, and asymmetric windows that are flush against walls. Beach houses all over the world have stolen from this style, and it can be found on steep slopes throughout the Bay Area.

All three traditions share many characteristics, including a disconnect between unpretentious exteriors—mountain cabins in the First Tradition, featureless boxes in the Second, "aw shucks, it just came out this way after we arranged all the rooms" in the Third—and interiors that delight. ◆

FACING AND ABOVE: With its walls of glass and low gable, Dailey's unassuming Price House appears to be from the early 1950s, not 1939. The house sprawls across a wooded site on the Peninsula. From the street side, it looks like just another rancher. Inside, the Price House is unpretentious, warm and woodsy—and very livable. The arrangement, size and height of the windows are all very Dailey. "It's very hard to get furniture into rooms," owner Jackie Gomez says, "because you're always blocking a window."

WORTH A LOOK

The Berliner House can be viewed from the street at 120 Commonwealth Avenue, San Francisco.

To see Dailey's more traditional side, visit the Spanish-style Allied Arts Guild, 75 Arbor Road, Menlo Park.

Tolman Hall (1962), on Euclid Street at the University of California–Berkeley, is not one of Dailey's more popular buildings but it has an appealing toughness.

Hertz Hall (1957), on the UC–Berkeley campus, is a great place to take in a concert. The lobby especially is very Dailey.

Dailey's Brazil Room was designed for the Golden Gate International Exposition of 1939, and then was transported to Tilden Regional Park in Berkeley, where it has become a popular spot for weddings. ◆

desk. "The day he died, that was in the afternoon, I came to see him in the morning. The table here was half full of little bits of keys. He said 'I've got to get it organized.'"

"That afternoon he went off the Golden Gate Bridge."

In the years since his suicide, Dailey has lost much of his fame and many of his buildings.

The Red Cross Building, which many regarded as among the best modern buildings in San Francisco, was demolished several years ago. In Santa Barbara, neighbors fought to preserve Dailey's Coral Casino from what they saw as an unsympathetic expansion. Todd Blake can point to two neo-Craftsman homes from his backyard in Ross that have recently replaced Dailey homes.

Ironically, Dailey's older, traditional homes are faring better than his modern ones because they better fit the temper of Peninsula home buyers. Bill Gomez expects his wonderfully unpretentious Dailey home will eventually be torn down for something splashier. "People just don't live in houses like this today in Atherton," he says.

But there are converts, like Tad and Dianne Taube, who own the 1939 De Bretteville estate in Woodside. When Tad first got a look at it, he saw wonderful oaks and land enough for a tennis court. The house itself he saw as a problem. "It's so ugly," he complained to an architect friend. "Can you think of something we can do to make it look better?"

"He said, 'If you want to [mess] up a Gardner Dailey design, get yourself another architect.'" Taube took another look and fell in love. "What I discovered," Taube says, "was I had stumbled into a real architectural jewel." ◆

GARDNER A. DAILEY (1895–1967)

Gardner Dailey and his younger colleague Joseph Esherick work at the drafting table. Photo courtesy of Environmental Design Archives, University of California–Berkeley.

Style: Dailey helped create "The Second Bay Tradition," blending International Style with local vernacular traditions.

Active: Between the late 1920s and 1967, Dailey designed about 200 residences primarily on the Peninsula and in San Francisco and Marin. He also designed schools and colleges as well as retail, commercial and office projects.

Other practitioners: William Wurster, John Dinwiddie, Joseph McCarthy and Clarence Mayhew also created modern Bay Tradition houses in the years before World War II. Dailey's style influenced many later architects, including those who designed homes for Joseph Eichler. Dailey's office was continued after his death by former associates and operates today as Levikow Associates. ◆

Nothing could be more rustic than the hallway serving the bedrooms, with its terra-cotta tile floor and exposed, white-washed beams of Douglas fir.

Middle-Class Modernism
Roger Lee Designed Homes for Every Man

Howard Bennett and Meng Yeo weren't committed to modernism when they sought an affordable home in the East Bay. But they did insist on a well-designed home with panache. "We wanted something with a recognizable style, something that had been designed, not just ad hoc," Bennett says.

Indoor-outdoor living, the mantra of California modernism, requires collaboration between architect and homeowner. Irene Wilkinson has played her part.

What they fell for was a modest home of glass and redwood designed by Roger Lee, whom his former colleague landscape architect Ted Osmundson remembers as "one of the best architects around."

Roger Yuen Lee (1920–1981) designed more than 100 houses, mostly in the East Bay but also throughout Northern California, Nevada and Hawaii. He came of age right after World War II, along with other architects who grew up with the ideals of European modernism that architecture should be functional, unadorned and elegant, and make a difference in the lives of everyday people.

The lesson was emphasized by their experience during the war, when architects designed war housing, barracks, airfields and factories using streamlined production techniques with an eye towards thrift and speed.

Lee served in Hawaii designing bunkers and other structures for the Army Corps of Engineers. After the war he worked in Los Angeles, and then with architect Fred Langhorst for two years before going out on his own.

Young architects emerged from the war energized. Home magazines filled their pages with articles about new techniques, materials and styles—plastics, aluminum, manufactured houses—for dream houses for returning GIs and their brides.

It was to be a new age with a new way of living, and modernism, with its clean lines, would make it work, people thought. In 1949 *Architectural Forum* devoted three pages to a cluster of six El Cerrito homes designed by Lee with the headline "Modern design: Out West the customer is starting to demand it."

Roger Lee built this house in Orinda for Robert and Irene Wilkinson, an engineer and landscape designer, fifty years ago with an eye on the environment. Cantilevered eaves keep out direct sun in the summer but let winter sun hit the interior brick wall for passive solar heating. The house is perfectly integrated with its setting.

The idea, Bennett says, was that "Working-class people aren't condemned to live in ugly places." Lee belonged to a generation of architects—the last—that custom-built modern homes for middle-class, even working-class, people. He influenced many younger architects and left the Bay Area with dozens of homes, although many rarely hit the market.

Irene Wilkinson, who has lived in a Lee home in Orinda for almost fifty years, keeps a waiting list of people who'd like to buy her house. She's met other owners of Lee houses—people associated with UC–Berkeley, members of the California Native Plant Society—who do the same.

Wilkinson, who knew Lee well, loves her house because it is unpretentious and harmonizes with nature. A landscaper, she has surrounded and filled it with bamboo and flowers, her collections of sea stones and shells, and plush animals. The architecture may be minimal but the décor is not. Although the house is entirely Wilkinson, it is also entirely Lee.

ROGER Y. LEE (1920–1981)

Style: "The Second Bay Area Tradition," also "redwood post and beam," a mid-century regional variant of modernism that borrowed influences from vernacular farmhouses. Open plans, glass walls, attention to nature.

Active: Northern California, late 1940s to the late '60s, mostly in the East Bay, especially Berkeley, Kensington and El Cerrito.

Known for: Lee designed rhythmic and distinctive modern homes of glass and redwood panels for people with limited budgets.

Other practitioners: John Funk, Henry Hill, Aaron Green, Donald Hardison and Vernon De Mars, and Eichler's architects—Anshen & Allen, Jones and Emmons, and Claude Oakland—were also active in the post–World War II years, designing homes for the middle class or subsidized housing for the poor. ♦

"You can identify one of his houses instantly when you see one," says Osmundson, of Theodore Osmundson & Associates, mentioning the generally flat roof (Wilkinson's has a low pitch), an inconspicuous front door and glass walls everywhere but the bedroom.

The homes are usually long and low, small (Wilkinson's is 980 square feet) but look larger, have no decoration other than lovely rhythms created by structural elements, ceiling beams and decking, and a strong Asian influence.

Lee's homes were post and beam—exposed beams supported by widely and regularly spaced posts. This technique, common to modern homes, provides for larger spaces and larger expanses of glass than are possible with traditional wood-frame construction.

Architect Paul Adamson and his wife live in a 1961 Lee home in Kensington that is part of a hidden, three-house complex. Lee called it a "studio home" because the 1,350-square-foot house is virtually a single room divided—or not—by doors that can quickly disappear. "It's one big volume," Adamson says. "It's a fantastic party house because people can be anywhere and see each other."

The house is almost a square, with a kitchen-dining area downstairs next to a living room that is separated by an accordion door from a "bedroom," which becomes part of the living room when the door is open. The master bedroom has a real door, but this is not so in the other upstairs room, which serves as their son's bedroom—and as a balcony overlooking the living room when its accordion door is open.

Bennett's home in El Cerrito is built on four-by-six-foot modules. The windows are that size, so are the wall panels, and so are the surprisingly boxy doors—an amusing touch. Bennett loves the simplicity of his house, and the clarity provided by the exposed posts and beams, which are used as visual as well as structural elements. "Literally you can see the structure from anywhere in the house," he says.

Lee used concrete-slab foundations with radiant floor heat, as in the tract homes of Joseph Eichler. Lee's houses bear some resemblance to Eichler's, and he shared some of the developer's commitment to providing good modern housing for the middle class. Lee himself partnered in several small developments, turning out neighborhoods of four or five houses. He also designed what he called the "Moduflex" house, based on standardized parts. Eichler used the same strategy to keep his costs down.

Darryl Roberson, principal of the San Francisco firm STUDIOS Architecture, who worked with Lee during the mid-1960s, says costs stayed low because their clientele had tight budgets, often $25,000. Lee could produce a house for $20 a square foot. "He had it down to a way of doing it that was really quite nice," Roberson says.

FACING: Paul Adamson's house in Kensington is pure modernism in the forest, a rectangle of posts and glass that carves out a section of the house to serve as an entry courtyard. ABOVE: Post and beams allow for an open plan and the almost complete elimination of walls in Wilkinson's house. Dining room and garden seem one.

But Lee paid attention to detail and his homes never looked cheap. From 1949, a year after he opened his own office, through the '60s, his homes were often written up in major architectural magazines. He was included along with Richard Neutra and William Wurster in articles about top

West Coast modernists, and within a few years he was in *House & Garden*, *Sunset* and other popular magazines.

Wilkinson's home, built on a shelf of land above a golf course, "was the cheapest construction you could build at the time," she says.

Irene and her late husband, Bill, an electrical engineer, met Lee when they moved into a rental unit at the home Lee built for himself in 1949 in flatland Berkeley. They became friends with Lee and his wife, Rena, and Lee helped them select their lot.

"The idea was to build it into the hill, not have one of those huge plaster jobs we have now, with the two-story front door," she says. "We did most of the work."

The living area—living room, small dining area, a kitchen hidden behind a freestanding storage unit—fireplace—is glass-walled on three sides. The other is a retaining wall that holds back the hill.

A glass-walled atrium separates the living area from two bedrooms. The effect is startling—looking around the home, it really is hard to tell what's inside and what's out. The atrium was designed to be converted into a bedroom, and Lee left plans for other additions. But the Wilkinsons were content. "We had two children," she says. "They just learned to get along."

Nor had they need for air-conditioning. The roof cantilever keeps out the sun in the summer but allows it

THE EICHLER PHENOMENON

BETWEEN THE EARLY 1950s and when he died in 1974, developer Joseph Eichler put more Californians into modern homes than any other builder.

Working with three architectural firms—Anshen & Allen, Jones & Emmons, and Claude Oakland Associates—he built 11,000 glass-walled, post-and-beam homes, primarily on the Peninsula and in Marin County but also in the East Bay. Eichler also built townhouses and high-rise housing in San Francisco. Eichler homes were aimed at middle-class buyers.

Eichler's houses succeeded functionally and aesthetically because he chose superb architects. Bob Anshen and

Stephen Allen ran a pioneering San Francisco modern firm. A. Quincy Jones and Frederick Emmons were prominent in Southern California. Oakland developed his skills while working as a designer with Anshen & Allen before going out on his own.

Eichlers remain beloved today for their openness, the woodsiness that comes from Philippine mahogany siding and open-beam ceilings, and for their atriums, a popular open-air room found in many models. Fans are fiercely loyal, and an entire industry has grown up around restoring and preserving Eichler homes.

FACING: Adamson's son has a mezzanine bedroom that opens to the living area through accordion doors, a wonderful effect but not conducive to privacy. ABOVE: Adamson's house is small but the living room is high; it has two stories of glass that let the stars in.

Lee loved floating fireplaces. Irene Wilkinson uses hers to display collectables from nature.

to hit the brick fireplace wall in the winter for passive solar heat throughout the day and night. Lee also made use of the golf course. On hot days, convection causes air to rise over the course and flow through their open windows, cooling things down, Wilkinson says.

Wilkinson loves such details as the fireplace, which hovers a foot above the floor, thanks to a cantilever "with enough steel in it for ten men to stand on it." If the fireplace rested on the floor, Lee told her, "'with a small room, your eye will stop at it.' Things like that Roger insisted on."

Bennett's house, built in 1952, occupies a sloping lot in the El Cerrito hills, but provides a level living area, thanks to a basement that is stepped into the hillside. The exterior is simple, taupe-colored board and batten. The glass-walled living room opens onto an outdoor living area that makes for great parties. The kitchen is just big enough for one person.

Bennett and Yeo bought the 1,700-square-foot home ten years ago from the widow of the man who built it, a cabinetmaker who had worked with Lee. "He was just a working guy so he didn't have lots of money."

Like most of the people who bought Lee's homes originally, Bennett and Yeo were first-time home buyers, moving from a rental in San Francisco.

"There's no decoration and no frou-frou about it," Bennett says. "It creates a stylish space. I like the fact that it was built for a working-class guy."

The Roger Lee that Wilkinson remembers was easygoing, sociable, a wonderful dancer. The Lees and Wilkinsons took ballroom dancing classes and showed off at the Claremont Hotel. She describes parties for family and friends at his second home, which he built in Kensington, furnished with Danish modern.

Lee, who grew up in Oakland, met his wife in Hawaii during the war, says his son, Roger Allyn Lee, a commercial photographer. The Bay Area had few Chinese American architects when Lee got his license in 1947.

Lee was a solid family man, raising two sons and a daughter in comfort, his son says. He enjoyed sports cars, took the family on long vacations every summer to Yosemite, Death Valley or Oregon, and loved to fish. Lee was a cagey gambler, Wilkinson remembers, playing blackjack just enough on their shared trips to Nevada to pay for the trip, and then leaving the table for good.

Lee's office in Berkeley had up to half a dozen architects and ten people total. By the mid-'60s he'd moved the

office to San Francisco. Besides homes, Lee and his associates designed apartments near campus, Lake Tahoe condos, several churches and occasional commercial projects. Lee and Osmundson drew up never-executed plans for a hotel and convention center for the then-barren Berkeley waterfront that called for more than fifteen buildings.

In Hawaii Lee continued to design modern homes, many of them larger than before and with shed-style roofs. He also designed a hospital and took up watercolors. He died of cancer in 1981.

Lee's name is no longer well known, but his homes have their followers. "It's nothing special, as they say," Bennett says of his. "Just a pretty, perfect, beautifully designed house." ◆

LEE HOUSES

Like many modern homes of their period, Lees are hard to appreciate from the street.

The **Wilkinson House** can be spotted at **440 Camino Sobrante**, Orinda.

One of Lee's "Moduflex" houses—the word came from "modern" and "flexible"—can be seen at **1714 Arlington**, El Cerrito.

A dignified Lee home is easy to see at **2081 Eunice Street**, Berkeley.

One of his typical, inconspicuous designs is at **6039 Chabolyn Terrace**, Oakland. ◆

All Natural
Jack Hillmer Likes His Wood Raw and His Spaces Spare

Jack Hillmer was already late for a meeting with a friend at the La Jolla Art Center when he spotted El Pueblo Ribera Apartments. He hopped off the bus to take a look. Architect Rudolph Schindler's cottages were among the first modern buildings Hillmer, a recent transplant from Texas, had ever seen. Two months later, a vacancy allowed him to move in. "I'd wake up in the morning," Hillmer recalls, "and it was wonderful looking at the sheen on the [redwood] ceiling."

The Cagliostro House turns its back on the street but presents plenty of street-side drama nonetheless, with a sheltered carport and immense cantilevered trellis. The siding is redwood.

Six years later, Hillmer was designing his own modern masterpieces, first with partner Warren Callister, and then on his own. The love of natural wood stayed with him.

"I don't like to use paint," Hillmer says. "I like to use the wood raw with no finish on it so you can see the sheen of the wood, the texture of the wood. Wax destroys the sheen. I prefer no finish at all."

Hillmer's use of natural materials helped define the Bay Region Style in the years after World War II. He quickly won fame, his homes reproduced in architecture magazines and popular magazines such as *Life*. His work was shown at the San Francisco Museum of Art (today the Museum of Modern Art). William Wurster, the dean of UC–Berkeley's school of architecture, invited him to teach.

Hillmer also won a reputation as a perfectionist. By 1960 *Architectural Forum* summarized his career as "20 years of practice [that] have produced few buildings but very expressive ones."

The magazine called his Stebbins House "a house full of small visual discoveries planned in long painstaking hours over a drafting board; even the light push buttons are set in neat clusters into the woodwork and are color-coded, replacing the usual switches and plastic-covered plate."

All told, Hillmer produced fewer than ten finished homes—but they have had an inordinate influence because of their purity and beauty, even spirituality.

"My approach to architecture was as an art," he says. "The approach of most other architects is as a business. I never really thought about how much money I was getting."

The Cagliostro House living room floats above its sloping site, and its ceiling floats above the room, thanks to clerestory windows and exterior piers. "It's like all that mass has generated a force field that's lifted the ceiling," Richard Ehrenberger observes. The rooms seem like interior extensions of the deck, not vice versa.

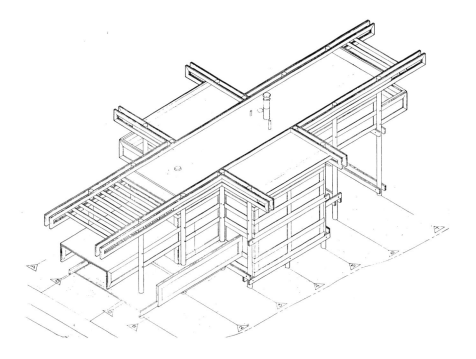

Erik Jepson, who decided to buy Hillmer's Cagliostro House in Oakland two minutes after walking inside, says of Hillmer's style: "It's a perfect marriage of two of the major movements of modern architecture, Frank Lloyd Wright organic architecture and the structuralism and functionalism of Mies van der Rohe. You can see the structure. Yet you're wrapped up in this warm redwood instead of concrete."

TOP: The materials of the Cagliostro House are rich, but the plan is ascetic. ABOVE: Hillmer doesn't like standard light switches. He uses buttons instead. FACING: Cabinets open at a touch.

Hillmer's homes are spare, poetic, relaxing in mood but rigorous in geometry. His expressive use of wooden beams, piers and siding recalls Japanese architecture and mountain lodges. His homes are solidly built, tough and masculine, rough-hewn and weathered—yet they seem to float, thanks to high bands of windows that separate the roof from the walls.

Standard framing, with vertical two-by-fours with external sheathing on one side and wallboard on the inside, was not for him. His redwood planks and panels do double duty as outside and inside sheathing. "My main thing is, the inside and the outside are identical, the same thing," he says.

Polished granite counters and glass-topped tables add elegance, and Hillmer hates exposed hardware. Electric sockets and hose attachments are hidden. Weeks after moving in, Jepson and his wife were still discovering storage areas that have no latches but open at the touch of a finger.

Hillmer's homes mix a Zen-like simplicity with a Baroque richness that comes not from ornamentation but from the beauty of the materials and the way the home interacts with the environment, framing dramatic views and filtering daylight. Walk up the entry steps in the Cagliostro House. If it's sunny outside, the light creates an echoing pattern of steps on the wall.

One characteristic bit of Hillmer drama is the bold cantilevering of roofs and decks. *Architectural Forum* called the cantilever of his Ludekens House in Belvedere "an arm saluting the bay."

Hillmer worked with a variety of materials. For the Ludekens House he visited a quarry near Fresno to choose thirteen tons of granite for the home's central core and fireplace. He often used concrete, but always "integrally colored"—iron oxides mixed into the concrete—not painted. Hillmer's Munger House was constructed of concrete blocks, a "do it yourself job" by the homeowner. The design, Hillmer says, was a spiraling hexagonal helix.

But wood is Hillmer's true material, in all its varieties, tones, textures and aromas. On warm days, the redwood boards in the Cagliostro House smell "like you're up in the Avenue of the Giants," Jepson says, "and the whole thing glows a beautiful brownish red."

JACK HILLMER (1918–)

Style: Hillmer developed a personal version of the modern Bay Region Style that emphasized expressive natural woodwork and rigorous geometric design.

Active: Hillmer designed fewer than ten completed homes between 1946 and the early 1990s. He also did many remodels.

Known for: Simple, meditative spaces, expressive and ornamental use of natural wood, solidly built homes that make the most of dramatic views.

Other practitioners: Warren Callister, Hillmer's former partner, has designed many homes with a similar expressive use of wood. ◆

Hillmer's Wright House in Inverness uses two-by-fours alternating with two-by-sixes to produce a ceiling that's a series of ridges and valleys. The home's complex plan of six-sided rooms creates odd, interpenetrating spaces and unexpected views. Like all of Hillmer's houses, the Wright is based on a strict geometric module, three and a half feet in this case, that regulates the spacing of columns and size of glass.

Hillmer, a straight-talking erudite man, is described by long-time friend and former student Richard Ehrenberger as "the highest order of aesthete I've ever encountered in my life."

The only child of a sheriff, Hillmer didn't find much artistic inspiration in his small Texas town nor much challenge in school. A trip to the Centennial of Progress in Chicago in 1933 exposed him to early versions of television and stereo sound. But what impressed him most was an immense redwood plank at the California exhibit.

He studied architecture at the University of Texas, where Warren Callister was a year ahead, because it was the closest program he could find to fine arts. Graduating just before World War II, Hillmer's career was put on hold while he designed bomber interiors in San Diego. The trusses that went into airplane wings later turned up in his Ludekens House, and wings also inspired his love of cantilevers.

Callister joined Hillmer in San Francisco after the

war. They convinced the owner of a real estate firm to give them an office rent-free in exchange for improvements. Their office became a meeting room for Telesis, a group of idealistic architects and planners. "One of our major interests was to make the world better," Hillmer says. He lived in the office, sleeping on a foam rubber mattress. "There was an excitement to it," Hillmer says of being an architect in San Francisco after the war. "It seemed like anything was possible."

Hillmer and Callister's landlord, Haines Hall, needed a home, owned a lot in Marin County and, just as importantly, had wood, which was hard to find and still controlled by wartime rationing. Hall had beautifully weathered boards from a ranch house and stables. Hall wanted a traditional house, but they would build only modern. Hall told the architects, "You can do whatever you want," Hillmer recalls. "We're only going to live in it a couple of years. If we don't like it, it won't destroy our lives."

To site the home, Hillmer says, "We climbed into the trees and, where we saw the view was best, we measured

LEFT: Black granite countertops absorb the sun during the daytime and keep life cozy at night. Transparent glass cabinets open the kitchen to dining area. Cabinets pop open for convenient storage. ABOVE: Glass shelves between kitchen and dining room slide into walls without hardware.

Jack Hillmer   111

down about five feet and made that the floor area." To preserve the many oaks, they punched holes in the roof for the trunks to pop through. Architects loved the house, the press wrote it up and the clients approved. "He lived there till he died," Hillmer says of Hall. "[His widow] still lives there."

Hillmer and Callister designed a few more projects that were never built, and then they split up. "I thought we would always work together," Hillmer says. "I was very devastated by that decision." For years they didn't speak.

Callister went on to design many woodsy and very personal homes, and to head a firm of more than fifty people that did such major projects as Rossmoor in Walnut Creek.

Hillmer never applied for an architecture license ("I didn't believe in controlling design"), never sought clients and sometimes rejected those who sought him. "I tried to have a client that I had a similar taste with really," he says. "And to spend so much time with a client, it's a year or more, I didn't want to spend that time with someone I didn't like."

Hillmer did some remodeling and additions, designed a metals factory in Los Angeles that was never built as he had planned, and conceived a house for an orthodontist that would resemble "a ruin that originally had been equally spaced columns everywhere but some were missing."

"I designed several buildings that didn't get built because I took too much time on it, too much perfection," he says.

During the 1950s and '60s, Hillmer taught at UC–Berkeley. Ehrenberger recalls the class as wildly popular. Hillmer helped form the Society for the Preservation of Golden Gate Park, which blocked plans to build a freeway through the Panhandle. Hillmer also helped restore the torii gates in San Francisco's Japanese Tea Garden.

FACING: Hillmer used the same materials inside and out, allowing the natural redwood to weather. Inside, it's reddish and roughly textured, and the effect is elegant yet rustic. ABOVE: The top floor of Hillmer's Cagliostro House is virtually a single space, very spare, combining wonderful wooden textures with a precise play of light.

HILLMERS TO SEE

The façade of the **Cagliostro House** can be admired at **49 Vicente Street**, Oakland.

His **Stebbins House** hides away at **75 Upland Road**, Kentfield. ◆

Hillmer briefly gave up architecture, and considered an acting career. He performed in a play on campus with Stacy Keach.

Over the years, Hillmer has lived, temporarily, in homes by many modern architects, including Frank Lloyd Wright and Bernard Maybeck. "I went through a period of house sitting," he says, "but only in good buildings."

One of Hillmer's last projects, in the 1990s, was replacing a house he had built earlier for Dominic Cagliostro, which was lost in the Oakland Hills fire. The second version was better than the first, he says, and is his favorite project.

Today Hillmer, who never married, shares a house with Callister, a widower. Hillmer enjoys cooking. They get out regularly to classical concerts. Hillmer still keeps an eye on his houses but doesn't always approve of how they have grown. "Most of my buildings have been altered in some ways which I'm not happy about, because they're my children," he says. ◆

Listening for Architecture
Warren Callister's Homes Arise from the Spirit of the Place

The editors at *House and Home* thought they had Warren Callister nailed. "You can tell Callister's homes," they told their readers in a lavish fourteen-page layout in 1962, "by the strong sculptural forms of his roofs . . . the interplay of straight and curved lines . . . the pervading sense of solid strength . . . the lofty and the dramatic interior spaces . . . the windows whose mullions are maximized."

But Callister, who is still doing architecture more than forty years later, doesn't believe his designs can be easily told. Ask about his style and he talks philosophy, place, climate, and client, and tells a few anecdotes. Then he denies designing buildings at all. "They manifest themselves," he says.

"I think I have a Callister way of going about it. I don't think of a style per se, but I do see that I repeat myself at times."

"It's not International Style. It's more regional in feeling," he says. "The work I do is trying to reflect the region I'm in."

Callister comes up with designs by walking the site and listening, a technique he learned from photographer Minor White. "You leave yourself open and it all starts flooding in," he says. "You're listening for more than superficial things. The most powerful things come in when you listen.

"Hearing is one of the most important things. It was subconscious, really. You listen to it and it tells you what's most important. It's like standing back from a painting and taking a longer view. You have to find the architecture. You don't come to it preconceived."

Callister remains best known for boldly modern custom homes that array wooden beams and panels rhythmically and expressively, and play up the drama. But his work includes some surprises, including bay-side homes that resemble ships, and trend-setting suburban communities that are modern in layout and spirit but often traditional in appearance.

His firm designed the first phases of Rossmoor, a sprawling retirement community in Walnut Creek, as well as large-scale projects on the East Coast. He even designed a never-built city for the Central Valley that would have preserved farmland by housing a million people in high-rise towers.

Many modern homes proclaim a less-is-more aesthetic. Not Callister's Duncan House, which he designed with associate Jack Payne, where three planks of wood are consistently used where one would do to create rhythm and interest, and where the two-story window that overlooks San Francisco from Twin Peaks is divided into three views by immense and deeply recessed wooden piers, each sculpted of multiple wooden members. Adding further drama to the house is a vaulted roof of laminated wood.

"Glassiness is not the character of these houses," *House and Home* observed. "On the contrary, weight and mass are often employed."

His expressive use of wood joinery recalls Japan and the work of Arts and Crafts architects Greene and Greene, and it is not surprising that Callister is also a sculptor.

"The house has two moods—party and cathedral," Dr. Gwen Evans says of the house, which was commissioned by her husband, Dr. Cloyce Duncan, in the late 1950s. "It

Callister's pleasure in laying post on beam and texture on texture recalls Arts and Crafts pioneers Greene and Greene, as well as Maybeck and other First Bay Tradition architects. This is the living room of the Duncan House.

really inspires meditation, creativity, abstract thought."

As his firm expanded, Callister moved beyond this "Bay Tradition" modernism, designing homes, apartments, condos and entire neighborhoods in a variety of styles—still modern in plan and outlook but recalling Nantucket cottages, New England barns or sheds.

In Sonoma, Callister designed a Moroccan-themed home that resembles adobe, with a wall that slides away to turn an indoor room into a veranda. One home in Tiburon reflects its bay-side location with portholes. He created several explicitly Japanese homes, with translucent panels, reed shades and tatami mats.

Callister claims to care as little about the concept of "modernism" as he does of "style"—though he brags about talking one client out of filling a New England field with faux-Tudor homes. But he does appreciate the influence of the Bay Tradition and attributes its characteristics to the balmy climate and influences from Japan.

Bay Tradition architects always sought a sense of place, which was avoided by International Style purists. Callister borrowed from regional styles even more freely than many of his contemporaries. Callister's work never lost its sense of rhythm, attention to detail, connection to place and humor. Architecture, he told an interviewer in 1966, should "make you weep, make you laugh." Architecture, he said, "is not building a shelter, but a mood, a feeling, a sense."

Born in Rochester, New York, and raised in Florida and Texas, Callister studied architecture because his scholarship only covered schools in Texas—and there wasn't a fine arts program among them. His studies at the University of Texas—architecture, sculpture and sociology—were interrupted by World War II, and he never got his degree.

Drafted into the army, he worked on the Alcan Highway in Alaska, designed barracks and officers' clubs with the Corps of Engineers, and then joined the Army Air Corps, where he flew B-17s and B-24s in the United States. His first sight of San Francisco was from the air.

After the war Callister brought his wife and son to San Francisco to join former University of Texas classmate Jack

CHARLES WARREN CALLISTER (1917–)

Style: Warren Callister (he doesn't use "Charles") has worked in the modern Bay Region Style and in more eclectic styles rooted in modern tenets since 1946.

Active: Callister and his firms designed several hundred homes and other projects from the late 1940s to the present.

Known for: Handcrafted, dramatic custom homes, and medium and large planned neighborhoods.

Other practitioners: His former partner Jack Hillmer is also known for the expressive use of wood. ◆

Hillmer in the firm Hillmer-Callister. Hillmer and Callister's first house, in Marin in 1946, won much attention. They designed two others that were never built, and then they split up.

Callister opened an office in Belvedere, sharing a building with the Belvedere Land Company, which developed the town and still owns and manages much property. He hit it off with the land company owners; it didn't hurt that both the Callisters and Allens were Christian Scientists, or that

Callister still talks about the first time he rode a cable car, and he was thinking of the shape of the cars when he and associate Jack Payne designed the vaulted roof of the Duncan House in Twin Peaks in 1959. The laminated wood for the ceiling was bent on-site. "We learned if you do it in the sun, they bend much more easily," Callister recalls. An atrium over the bar leads to the master bedroom.

ABOVE: A separate vault spans the entry hall. FACING: Only the Duncans's garage faces the street—but it suggests that the house is very special.

Mary Frances Callister had gone to school with Betty Allen. Over the years Callister did many buildings for the land company and for individual clients throughout town.

After a few years, the firm moved into two old railroad storehouses overlooking the bay in Tiburon. Callister was part of the artistic and literary crowd that hung out in Sausalito and Tiburon. One of his clients was the mystical painter Gordon Onslow-Ford.

Callister always worked with partners because he enjoyed collaborating and because he never sought an architect's license. "It's like licensing artists. How do you do that? This is a genuine artist, and this is not a genuine artist?" he says, and laughs. (He was finally awarded a license on his seventieth birthday.) His firms included Callister & Payne; Callister, Payne & Bischoff; Callister, Payne & Rosse; and Callister, Gately & Heckman.

Being an architect, Callister says, is as collaborative as being a film director. "Suddenly you discover you're placing people and making up the group that will do the projects. And that's a form of design too."

Asia influenced Callister's way of doing things as well as his style. During a trip to Asia with a client in 1966, he was impressed by the Asian "art of doing." "They sort of tolerated the finished work," he says, "but the great part of it was the ceremony. The tea ceremony—it's not drinking the tea. It's the ceremony."

Equally influential were social theorists like Lewis Mumford, who believed that improving man's habitat would improve man himself, and the film *The City*, which

impressed Callister both for its message and its Aaron Copland score. In the 1950s Callister belonged to Telesis, a group of architects and planners dedicated to regional planning.

By the mid-1960s, his firm of fifty people, with offices in Tiburon and Amherst, Massachusetts, was designing tract homes for developers, spec homes and entire communities. Callister's advice to tract developers: "Design and build each house with a strong, bold form," reflect regional tradition, simplify, use only one exterior material and only one kind of door. Several of the projects were featured in popular and trade magazines as examples of modern California-style planning that could be successfully replicated anywhere.

At Heritage Village in Connecticut, gabled models had names like "Mark Twain," "Villager," "Carriage House" and "Ethan Allen." The homes were low-slung, and fit into the landscape, and the trees were preserved.

Callister's firm did its own land planning. "New developments were usually pretty rigid," Callister says. "We were clustering the houses in a different way."

Callister understood that architecture could affect social dynamics. Common gardens were provided, and homes were arrayed in groups of no more than fifteen. "If it gets larger than that, it's like an apartment building," he says.

Rossmoor in Walnut Creek, a retirement community built in the 1960s, won Callister national attention. "A harmony of land planning and architecture that is unprecedented in a complete town," the trade magazine *House and Home* wrote.

The homes—mostly four- to eight-unit condos and co-ops—that Callister designed for Rossmoor's early phases remain intact, as do portions of his community centers and art rooms. The architecture ranges from Bay Tradition modern—broad eaves over board-and-batten siding—to more eclectic, including mini-mansard roofs. Callister's firm designed roughly 3,000 units on 600 acres.

In the mid-1960s, Callister designed his most ambitious development ever, a city for 250,000 people in immense towers that look suspiciously like the wooden piers in the Duncan House. The goal was to provide high-density living while preserving open space. It was never built.

ABOVE: The McMurray House has an exterior of stucco, redwood trim and a concrete-tile roof. Callister dislikes looking at gutters and downspouts. Rainwater is channeled to the ground through pipes hidden in the walls. McMurray finds the sound comforting. BELOW, RIGHT: A Buddha greets visitors at the entry to the McMurray House. FACING: McMurray collects Asian art, and the house has Asian proportions and a suggestion of rice paper walls. Callister provided several *tokonoma*, Japanese niches for the display of art.

But Callister never got too big to turn out another house.

A friend suggested Jim McMurray call Callister after losing his house in the 1991 Oakland Hills fire. "I don't think Callister wants to design a little house for me," McMurray said. But he called, and Callister visited the burned-out site and asked questions—stiffly.

"He asked how I felt about my house before. I liked it. It was a nice house. But it's not a Callister house. All of a sudden he got a big smile on his face and said 'Let's talk.'"

Soon Callister was hovering over the site, lunching with the workmen on a ledge fifty feet above the ground, arguing with the painters over color, and adjusting windows to make room for one of McMurray's Asian screens.

The result is a symphony of redwood, mahogany and knotty pine, with Sheetrock held in place like Oriental panels. The living-dining area is arched and held up by paired posts, and the shape of the hillside provides an asymmetrical rhythm that is echoed in the pitch of the roof, the shape of windows and a hanging lamp.

"To me, that's like a stroke of genius," McMurray says. "One thing might be an accident. But you duplicate it over and over again. It worked well."

Today Callister shares a home with Jack Hillmer at Bahia, a bay-side development he and Payne designed in Novato. One of his sons is a builder, another is an architectural photographer.

His firm is now a one-man operation. Part-time assistants handle the computer drafting. He's doing a guest house, a remodel and a church in Santa Cruz with a catenary roof that recalls waves on the sea. "This church we're doing down there," he says, "the whole thing is coming together like magic."

He misses the camaraderie of the old days, however. "People come back and say it was the greatest time of our lives," he says. "I don't think we realized it so much, but we were having fun, we were having a great time." ◆

CALLISTERS TO CATCH

Callister's houses have a spiritual air, as do his churches, which are easier to visit.

The **First Church of Christ Scientist at 501 San Rafael Avenue,** Belvedere, from 1950, is his first and evokes sails from nearby boats.

The chapel at Mills College, **5000 MacArthur Boulevard,** Oakland.

First Church of Christ Scientist, 279 Camino Alto, Mill Valley.

First Unitarian Church at 1187 Franklin, at Geary, is a beautiful small chapel and offices. Done with Payne and Martin Rosse.

Two of his homes can be spotted in the Berkeley hills, at **2625** and **2637 Rose Street.** ◆

The colors are rich, the wood varied, the plan simple in Jim McMurray's living area upstairs, in this house designed by Callister in the Oakland Hills. Three segments of skylights along the roof ridge define living, dining and kitchen areas. Callister designed the hanging lamp, whose asymmetric shape is echoed in the window beyond and in the shape of the hills outside. Callister stole the colors from McMurray's Asian rugs. "The painters were rather upset," McMurray remembers. "They wanted white walls."

Donald and Helen Olsen's décor includes classic black leather UNESCO chairs, two chairs by Marcel Breuer, a sofa designed by George Nelson, and a white harpsichord built by the couple's son, Alan, as a teenager. The floor is oak, and the ceiling is Douglas fir painted white.

Against the Grain
Donald Olsen Kept His Modernism Pure

Architect Donald Olsen understood that he was a different sort of Bay Area modernist. And his boss made sure everyone else did too.

"He'd introduce several people correctly," Olsen says of William Wurster, dean of architecture at UC–Berkeley, "and then when he got to me, he'd say with a straight face, 'And now I want to introduce you to the Other Point Of View.'" Then Wurster, who considered himself dean of Bay Area architecture as well as of the school, would walk off without mentioning Olsen's name.

Modern architecture in the Bay Area has become identified with the Bay Tradition, or Bay Region Style, a softer, woodsier, self-consciously regional variant of the Modern Movement that traces its roots to Maybeck's quirky brown-shingled proto-modernism and absorbed the same environmental consciousness. Olsen was never part of it. He's a pure International Style modernist in the tradition of the German Bauhaus designers of the 1920s: Walter Gropius, Mies van der Rohe and Le Corbusier. He is one of a small handful of Bay Area architects to work in the style.

Both Bay Tradition and International Style (or Modern Movement, as its practitioners prefer) use open plans with free-flowing space and walls of glass, and both styles promote the belief that good architecture can help reshape society. But where a Bay Tradition home would generally use natural redwood, International Style opted for white paint over wood, or stucco or concrete. Bay Tradition homes evoke barns, mountain cabins, and the history and

Peter Selz's book-lined study provides views into the living area. The large painting is Sam Francis's *Iris;* in the corner is a sculpture by Stephen de Staebler.

traditions of the region. International Style homes, some proponents claim, evoke nothing from history or geography. They are abstract boxes equally at home on a Paris boulevard or a Berkeley hillside.

The differences were aesthetic and emotional and could generate heat. Olsen remembers when a Bay Tradition landscape architect stopped by the Kip House, under construction in the Berkeley Hills, with an exterior of all-heart redwood. The landscaper made a few suggestions for plants.

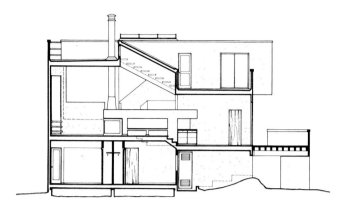

LONGITUDINAL SECTION LOOKING EAST

ABOVE: A roof deck above and an enclosed deck on the main living room allows for easy gardening and taking in the view. FACING: Olsen's house in Berkeley for art historian and curator Peter Selz is a series of interlocking spaces and odd angles, ideal for showing modern art.

Then Olsen said: "'I thought it would be good to inform you that the house is going to be painted white.' He stopped in his tracks and said 'No! No! No, no, no!' He said, 'You can't paint redwood.' I said, 'It takes a wonderful paint job.' What he meant was, morally you can't paint redwood."

Bay Traditionalists may consider the International Style cold, haughty, theoretical and lifeless. But when Olsen criticizes the Bay Tradition, he doesn't say the homes are too warm, informal or lively. He says they're boring and lack spatial drama and surprise. "The Bay Area style stuff was just an ordinary house gussied up a little bit," he says, though there are Bay Tradition architects whose work he admires, including Maybeck and Jack Hillmer.

What he prefers, Olsen says, is "a house with some zing, some sex to it," a house that is "fun, zestful to live in."

Close to fifty houses designed by Olsen provide the Bay Area with its largest residential dose of pure modernism. Unlike Los Angeles, which was introduced to International Style modernism in the 1920s by European architects Rudolph Schindler and Richard Neutra, the Bay Area never really took to the style. "That's one reason why Donald Olsen never had so many commissions, actually," says art historian

Peter Selz, who had Olsen build him a house in 1969.

Olsen spent thirty-six years teaching at UC–Berkeley's architecture school, often focusing more on epistemology and the limits of rationality than design. "People always asked me what that had to do with architecture," he says. "In a general sense, it had to do with everything and anything."

He ran his small (usually one associate) practice in the morning, and sometimes went years with few projects. Besides houses, he also designed some retail, office and multifamily units. Olsen is as hard a critic of his own work as he is of others, and counts only eight or ten of his houses as fully successful. "A great number of them were OK," he says, "but they weren't something I had total control over."

A full-blown Olsen house is rigorous in geometry, filled with light from walls of glass, narrow clerestory windows and skylights, glistening white exteriors splashed with panels of color, surprising shifts of space and occasional nautical touches. Windows are placed for dramatic lighting effects. Olsen enjoys spiral staircases and ramps. Many of his homes use structural steel, though he's never built an all-steel house due to cost.

Olsen would begin work on a house by producing many small, quick sketches, thoughts emerging from the pencil. He likes to have fun with his designs, and isn't always pure.

He has designed homes with deliberate historic references, including a hilltop mansion for an Italian American family that connected the outdoor swimming pool with the living areas by running a canal between the dining room and kitchen. "What a marvelous thing for a carnival of Venice," Olsen says. He even proposed an electric gondola. The project was never built.

Olsen's clients tended to be academics, their budgets limited, their sites challenging, their need for flexibility great.

For his next-door neighbors, the Kips, Olsen squeezed a split-level vertical box onto a steep site. The living room is a mezzanine above the dining-kitchen areas, all forming a single space with wonderful play of space and line. The bedrooms are a few steps down. No space is wasted on

The Olsen House looms in all its stark whiteness above Berkeley's wooded Hinkel Park. At night, the house glows.

hallways. Subtle touches include small windows hidden behind the fireplace, curved walls in the master bedroom, and ocean liner–style stair railings. A square deck juts over the street from the home's white face, its bottom painted a deep red to startle passersby.

"It has a centering feeling for me, this house," Joan Kip says.

Olsen's playful use of color comes out in the Birge House, built as part of Wurster's Greenwood Common development in Berkeley. It is Olsen's only natural redwood-clad home. Exposed beams in the living room are in subtle shades of brown, green and gold, and in the bedroom,

hanging cabinets form a Mondrian-like composition of grey, orange, yellow, blue and purple.

For Selz's home, Olsen designed three split levels, each with its own deck, and with a rooftop deck offering views of the Bay. "How come we have this Mediterranean climate," he asked Selz, "and nobody ever uses the roof?"

From the roof, an arched clerestory window gives a view of the living room, with its angled yellow ceiling. The home provides Selz with a book-lined mezzanine study, space for an extensive art collection, and a forum for parties.

Many of Olsen's clients wanted homes that were expandable as their families and incomes grew. Several have had unfinished basements turned into living areas. Olsen expanded his own home by glassing in decks for added interior space. But any client who remodels, or even paints, without Olsen's say-so is asking for trouble.

"I think his houses are his children and he never lets them go," Kip says. She remembers when he ordered workers to stop when he spotted them adding exterior lights at an unappealing angle. "I said 'Donald, this is not your house. It's my house.'" But she had the workers do as Olsen said.

Olsen, a talkative man who'll answer a question about architecture by discussing the limits of Hegelian historicism, is a fan of grand opera, travel and the philosophy of science. He considers his studies with philosopher Karl Popper in London as "my only real education." Bookshelves fill every room in his house, including the bathroom. An accomplished photographer, he has traveled the globe, photographing buildings he admires, which often differ markedly from his own.

He approached Gottfried Bohm's concrete Brutalist church in Neviges, Germany, expecting little, and found a modern church interior that was pitch black. "What I could see I certainly wanted pictures of that. It was disturbingly wonderful."

"It had the sense of being so enormous. What was the first thing that came to mind? Edmund Burke with his famous essay on the sublime and the beautiful."

Olsen grew up in Minneapolis, the son of a heating and air-conditioning contractor, and studied architecture at the University of Minnesota, a progressive school that focused on modernism. He graduated with a scholarship for graduate study at Harvard, where Walter Gropius was dean, but it was 1941. Kaiser Shipyards in Richmond needed architects. "I designed more buildings in three years than all the rest of my life put together": shops, railroad stations, cafeterias, a fire station. He met and married Helen Ohlson, a graphic artist from his hometown.

After the war, Olsen studied at Harvard with Gropius, which led to a job in Michigan with Finnish modernist Eero Saarinen. Olsen remembers architectural ideas pouring

DONALD E. OLSEN (1919–)

Style: International Style, as developed in Europe in the 1910s and '20s. Flat roofs, rectangular or curved massing, white stucco, walls of glass, no applied decoration, "functional" aesthetic.

Active: Olsen built homes in the East Bay, San Francisco and Marin from the early 1950s to 2001.

Known for: Elegant, economical homes that provide beautiful spaces, splashes of color and subtle humor.

Other practitioners: The Bay Area has never taken to the International Style. Gardner Dailey, Don Knorr and Raphael Sorriano created Modern Movement houses in the Bay Area, as did Los Angeles–based Richard Neutra. ◆

from Saarinen as a constant stream of doodles. When General Motors killed the project, the Olsens returned to the Bay Area.

Olsen's first-built houses were a pair in Orinda in 1951. Olsen worked for a few firms, including Wurster Bernardi & Emmons in San Francisco, and then he decided corporate life wasn't his style. He hung out a shingle. "I was the world's worst self-promoter," he says.

He never thought being a sole practitioner would be easy. He almost got a job designing embassies for the State Department in the 1950s. "That was the one big chance of a lifetime there," he says. His second came when Wurster invited him to teach.

Olsen's work was widely praised and published in architectural and popular magazines throughout his career, and he has many admirers. He retired from the university in 1990. His last house was designed in the mid-1990s and completed in 2001.

Olsen's home remains a Berkeley Hills landmark, a glass box floating above wooded Hinkel Park. The Kip

WORTH A LOOK

The Olsen and Kip Houses share a prominent hillside above Hinkel Park in Berkeley, **771** and **775 San Diego Road.** ◆

House is to one side, another Olsen design is to the other. Floor-to-ceiling glass surrounds the house, and the living area drapes are rarely closed.

Inside are the requisite black-and-brown leather modernist chairs, the architect's clutter, a mural by painter Claire Falkenstein along the spiral stairs. The centerpiece of the room is a white harpsichord, created years ago by the couple's son, Alan. To one side is a life-size statue of a Greek goddess, like something you'd see on a monumental Beaux-Arts slab of a building from 1898.

"Olsen clearly loves his house. It's his showpiece, you know," Joan Kip says, "and he lives in it as such, very much."

Walk by at night, and the house glows. ◆

Donald and Helen Olsen's living area is open to the world and overlooks a live oak–shaded creek outside. The drapes are rarely closed.

David Weingarten and Lucia Howard's Lafayette home pays homage to Bay Area architecture. Gothic tracery suggests Bernard Maybeck. Authentic gargoyles add to the effect. Stairs from the original home, a lodge designed by Lilian Bridgman, wind down behind the fireplace.

Telling Stories
Ace Architects Tips Its Hat to Architectural Tradition

There often comes a time during the building of an Ace house—perhaps the architects proposing a living room that resembles a cave, or partner David Weingarten's insistent booming laugh—when a client thinks, "Wait!" For Georgetta Beck it came when she saw the colors for her kitchen: teal, purple, yellow, green. "I thought, 'Oh God, what are we getting into?'"

Over the past twenty-five years Ace Architects, a partnership between Weingarten and Lucia Howard, has provoked many "Oh God" moments. It started in architecture school at the University of California–Berkeley, when they told professors and fellow students they wanted to design buildings that told stories. "They asked, 'Why would you even want to do that?'" Howard remembers.

"The subject comes from the site," Weingarten says of the stories, "it comes from the client, it comes from your imagination. It makes you think about things beyond the building itself. And you try to make it a very rich thing. It's not a one-liner."

"For us," he says, "a lot of the design part is figuring out what the subjects are and rendering them in ways that are more or less unmistakable, representational as opposed to abstract."

"We're always looking for the unusual things, the site or the clients, or circumstances that would make one place different than any other place."

Neighbors and passersby have been exasperated, delighted, and occasionally infuriated by Ace projects, including the Oakland Hills home shaped like a saxophone and Ace's own port-side office building, whose

Dixie Jordan's Oakland home has a pointed-arch living area shaped like Maybeck's long-gone Hearst Hall at the University of California. To its left is "Rapunzel's Tower."

story involves a sea serpent wrestling with a battleship.

But that battle pales when compared to Ace's Snake fiasco—or triumph—which unfurled in the far-from-unflappable town of Berkeley, when seemingly overnight a boring bank turned into storefronts that the *Oakland Tribune* suggested were designed by Ming the Merciless. "Silver snakes with forked tongues slither from its roof," Susan Stern reported. "The walls are the color of orange Pez and aging grapefruits."

"I suggest slapping fins on it and driving it away—but not before chaining David Weingarten, Ace Architects and the planning commission to the exhaust pipe," one citizen wrote. People threw tomatoes at it, and the city tightened its design review laws.

"It hit some button in Berkeley, which caused an explosion," Weingarten says, with another booming laugh. The project cost them some jobs short-term, Weingarten says, but added to their fame.

One story Ace tells in many of its works is the development of Bay Area architecture, emphasizing the woodsy, playfully eclectic architects of the First Bay Tradition—but not forgetting one of the founders of the so-called Third Bay Tradition, the late Charles Moore, Weingarten's uncle. (Weingarten traveled in Europe with "Uncle Chuck" as a child and did grunt work on his jobs.) Ace buildings include playful classical details suggesting Willis Polk, Gothic tracery a la Maybeck, who seems to be Ace's touchstone, and interlocking vertical spaces that recall Moore.

An early duplex on Telegraph Hill (Weingarten lived in the bottom unit) recapitulated the tale of Bay Area building vertically, first generation below, second and third upstairs. The first two floors recall the playful classicism

The living area's immense ceremonial space may not be efficient, but Jordan loves it. The pendant lamps repeat the form of the roof, the fireplace has a center art tile that was rescued from Jordan's earlier house on the site, which burned in the Oakland Hills fire. The balcony is Maybeckian and popular with young people. "Every kid who comes in here has to do *Romeo and Juliet*," Jordan says, "no matter how tough they think they are."

ACE ARCHITECTS: DAVID WEINGARTEN (1952–) AND LUCIA HOWARD (1951–)

Style: Ace works in a playful style allied with post-modernism that deliberately recalls Bay Tradition architects from years past.

Active: Since 1981 Ace has created dozens of homes, stores, offices and more, mostly in the Bay Area.

Known for: Buildings that are whimsical, filled with color and tell stories.

Other practitioners: Ace owes some of its wit to Charles Moore, Weingarten's uncle and an inventor of the Third Bay Tradition. ◆

of Willis Polk. The top unit has windows that suggest second-generation architect William Wurster, and an aedicula, a niche-like "house" within a room, a conceit of third-generation designer Charles Moore.

Although Ace has done stores and offices, amusement parks, and block after block of quirky storefront renovations, homes remain a mainstay. "The kinds of subject matters you develop in houses are especially rich," Weingarten says. "That's why we like to do them the best. They can get to be, and they should be, interesting and complex, but also subtle and alarming in the ways that people who inhabit them are. They become the most involved and compelling, and deepest form of architecture."

Ace's stories, Weingarten says, add a psychic dimension, a sense of comfort, to the home. "If you think of

ABOVE: A gold-domed tower adds a touch of exotica to the Beck-Miller House. FACING: Spanish revival with a twist describes the Beck-Miller House in Corte Madera, with its courtyard and carp pond.

houses you don't like, part of what makes places inhospitable is that there's nothing really special about them," he says. "One place becomes like another. It could be any place in the world."

Homes are more than stories, and Ace homes work. Georgette Beck loves her kitchen and its colors and her architects, who are adding another wing to the Corte Madera home she shares with her husband, Eric Miller. "When you work with David, you've got to trust him," Beck says, adding, "We were nervous about everything. He's been vindicated."

Debra Kirschenbaum loves the "swoop" that Ace designed for her kitchen remodel, a ribbon of blue turquoise glass that starts out as a stove hood, shoots across the ceiling "like smoke," and then descends to serve as the kitchen island. She equally appreciates how well the kitchen functions.

"For the most part it's pretty practical," says Dixie Jordan of her 1,400-square-foot house, with its "Rapunzel Tower" for her daughter, small master bedroom and kitchen, and cavernous two-story, Gothic-arched living room with Maybeck-style tracery that echoes Maybeck's Hearst Hall. (Hearst Hall burned in a 1922 fire, and so did Jordan's first house on the site, during the 1991 Oakland Hills fire.)

"We laughed a lot during the whole process," Jordan says, recalling how the architects' personalities played off each other. "Lucia gives you a sense of calm, like, there really will be a building when this is all done."

Although Ace claims not to have a style—especially not postmodernism—the firm has signatures. Their homes look like sculptures, with colliding masses that mesh or clash, circles playing off rectangles, and lots of free-form curves. Beck and Miller's home is laid out as a series of

curves that are sections of an immense circle. The curves define a line of palms, the shape of their carp pond, and the arc of the home's interior gallery.

Inside an Ace house, ceiling heights vary dramatically and spaces are tied together playfully, often by a vertiginous spiral staircase that Weingarten has patented. The stairs are often encased in a silo. Adding to the agribusiness motif is Ace's occasional use of barn doors, sometimes as interior doors. Bedrooms are often high above living areas. Or bedrooms are a level beneath the living areas, as in Weingarten and Howard's own home. Skylights and windows provide odd perspectives. From their bed, Beck and Miller can look at the fireplace burning in the living room below through two floor-level Spanish grille openings.

Like many Ace houses, the Beck-Miller has a flavor of Spain, with its red-tile roof and Moorish scalloping over windows and doors. What Miller originally had in mind was Santa Barbara Spanish Revival, circa 1925. "What he added to it was a modern twist," Miller says of Weingarten. Beck, a

TOP: A spiral staircase is an Ace trademark. This one leads to a bedroom overlooking Beck and Miller's living area.
ABOVE: Georgetta Beck's kitchen shares a single space with dining and living areas, and is richly colored.

The twelve-foot living area of the Beck-Miller House offers garden views. The ceiling designs recall Spanish Revival stenciling. The ceiling is resawn plywood. Weingarten designed the lighting fixtures.

New Yorker who was more interested in something fun than something Spanish, used to call the house "Casa Coney Island."

A line of spec houses along Skyline Boulevard in Oakland provides a modern take on the playful 1920s stucco Period Revival architecture that fills so many Bay Area suburbs, and the entirety of San Francisco's Sunset District, with various turrets, moat-crossing bridges, tile roofs, porthole windows and parapeted balconies.

It's not surprising that children love Ace architecture—or that Ace's largest job to date is rebuilding Children's Fairyland in Oakland. Their work is whimsical, not ironic.

This, more than anything, distinguishes it from mainstream postmodern. "I've always liked the goofy stuff," says Howard, who grew up in Tennessee where her great-uncle designed Storybook houses.

On an Ace house, dragon heads may decorate the ends of beams. Gargoyles, some rescued from Beaux-Arts skyscrapers, decorate interiors and courtyards. Weingarten's furniture wears animal heads.

As a result, Weingarten says, not everyone wants an Ace house. "But there are a few," he says, "and that is a perfect number." Today, he says, "We have people we say 'no' to. That's different than the old days. We took everything."

After graduating in 1977, Weingarten and Howard did a few jobs together: a small office for a friend of Weingarten's father in Carmel, a spec house in Beverly Hills, drafting for engineering firms. They formed Ace in 1981. "The reason we're 'Ace Architects,'" Howard says, "is we like the literalism and the many different historical connotations of Ace of Spades. It's the winning card, and also the death card. A lot of people connect to it."

An early remodel, for Howard's father in Tennessee, was an entry portico that looked like a house of cards. They won notice, and jobs, by designing a colorful gelateria and a deli in Oakland, using spiraling culvert pipes as hyper Italian columns. "Boy, we really love the delicatessen," a commercial developer told them, "because the pipes look good and they must have been really cheap."

Ace received timely help from Weingarten's father, the late Sol Weingarten, a lawyer and developer in Monterey, who helped bankroll Leviathan, their office building, and the Telegraph Hill house. Sol had provided similar help to his brother-in-law Charles Moore.

Ace remains a small firm, with four or five employees, and does two dozen projects a year, "from the insanely small to not very big," Weingarten says. One current project is five prefab homes, each given that "Oh God" treatment, for a nonprofit developer in West Oakland.

On the outside of the Howard-Weingarten House, the feel is very Spanish.

ACE PROJECTS

Children's Fairyland at 699 Bellevue Avenue, Oakland, a historic amusement park that Ace is restoring and re-creating, is the firm's largest project so far and is ongoing. www.aceland.com/news.html

Dixie Jordan's daughter may glare at tourists from her roost in Rapunzel's Tower at **6356 Broadway Terrace**, Oakland, but the house has become a landmark.

A group of spec homes on **Skyline** are worth a drive-by visit: numbers **7525, 7535, 7575, 7585** and **8047**.

Ace has transformed several commercial strips by supplying amusing new storefronts, including a stretch of **23rd Street in San Pablo** just west of San Pablo Avenue.

Ace's offices are in the Leviathan, **330 Second Street**, Oakland, California. ◆

Another work in progress is their own home. Weingarten and Howard bought a 1929 home designed by Lilian Bridgman, a First Bay Tradition follower of Maybeck, as a country retreat in Lafayette. The home, with brick and redwood walls and a breezeway between the bedrooms and living room, has been restored. The addition includes Gothic quatrefoils, a medieval gargoyle fragment, and demons decorating exterior beams. The pool is on a line with Mount Diablo, which provides the home with much of its story.

"The style of the house is kind of ranch Gothic," Weingarten says. Gothic, he notes, was a leitmotif of the First Bay Tradition architects, like Maybeck. "It's part of the First Bay style nobody dares do anything with anymore. People have latched onto the Arts and Crafts tendency. But nobody has taken Gothic to heart."

Ace may be quirky, but Weingarten and Howard claim fealty to the Bay's architectural tradition. "Yes, we're the last ones, we're dinosaurs," Weingarten says, and laughs. "In reality there are lots of Bay Region—style architects, but I think we're the only ones to own up to it." ◆

Sources

Lists of buildings for each architect were compiled by the Foundation for San Francisco's Architectural Heritage (Heritage), Berkeley Architectural Heritage Association (BAHA), the Napa County Historical Society, the Palo Alto Historical Association, and other historical groups. Gary Goss, an independent researcher, compiled some of the lists at Heritage and BAHA, working from building records and from photos, articles, notices and ads in such contemporary publications as *Architect and Engineer Magazine, California Architect and Building News*, and *Pacific Builder & Engineer*.

The Environmental Design Archives at the University of California, Berkeley, also provided lists of buildings, based on their collections of architect's drawings, plans and original files. Applications for National Register of Historic Places and other landmark designations have also proven useful.

Samuel and Joseph Cather Newsom

Samuel and Joseph Cather Newsom: Victorian Architectural Imagery in California, 1878–1908, by David Gebhard, Harriette Von Breton and Robert W. Winter, 1979.

Much of the biographical material came to author David Gebhard from the late Samuel Newsom Jr., Samuel Newsom's son. Heather Galanis, a descendant, supplied me with more information she had learned from Samuel, including the information that Archie Newsom was not a relation.

Margaret Edwards, a grand-niece of the brothers, wrote a master's thesis about their work in 1972 that also drew upon some family lore. *The History of the Newsom Brothers: California Architects and Publishers, 1852–1908*, San Jose State.

Samuel Newsom's article about California Missions appeared in the magazine *Overland* (October 1907). His article on the Castro Home in El Cerrito ran in the same publication in August 1908.

Leola Hall

BAHA has files on Leola Hall filled with news clippings, and displays several of her paintings, including *Miner's Cabin in the Sierras* and *Storm Clouds, Mount Diablo*. Located at 2318 Durant Avenue. Phone: 510.841.2242.

Ernest Coxhead

Berkeley Architectural Heritage Association has a file on Coxhead and a guide to his buildings in Berkeley.

Richard Longstreth's *On the Edge of the World: Four Architects in San Francisco at the Turn of the Century*, deals with Coxhead, Willis Polk, Bernard Maybeck and A. C. Schweinfurth.

Bay Area Houses, edited by Sally Woodbridge, and *Toward a Simpler Way of Life: The Arts And Crafts Architects of California*, edited by Robert Winter, include material on Coxhead.

UC–Berkeley's Environmental Design Archive has biographical material, including newspaper clippings and magazines that reprinted some of Coxhead's letters from France.

Helen McFarland, Coxhead's granddaughter, supplied biographical information, clarifying how Coxhead's wife died, not in childbirth, as reported by Longstreth, but after suffering an ache in her chest that may have been cancer. She also revealed that Coxhead summered in a home of his design in Inverness.

Luther Turton

The Napa County Historical Society, located in Turton's Goodman library, has Historic Resources Inventory reports on many of Turton's buildings.

Albert Farr

Historian Bradley Wiedmaier, who has written about Farr for Heritage, supplied biographical material and a listing of his buildings, including the home where Farr lived in Piedmont. Gail Lombardi of the Piedmont Historical Society has researched the Piedmont Farr houses in official records and architectural publications.

The California Department of Parks and Recreation has Historic Preservation certification applications at its Central Records Office in Sacramento for Farr's Benbow Inn, Phillipsburg-Riverwood Mansion in Ben Lomond, cottages and other buildings at Aetna Springs resort in Napa County.

John Hudson Thomas

Dick Riemann, who bought Thomas's Kensington House from the architect's son, John Wickson Thomas, learned from "Wick" that Thomas enjoyed strolling from home to Kensington's nearby shopping district, and that Thomas was reserved and idealistic.

The house came with many of Thomas's plans and drawings, the bulk of which Riemann donated to the University of California–Santa Barbara. Some drawings and plans remain, as do many books. An examination of Thomas's workroom and library suggests his meticulous work habits and enjoyment of the antique.

Several of Thomas's relations, including grand-nephews Chris Thomas and Mike Hearn, and Penny Adams, a grand-niece by marriage, provided information about the house in Diablo, and about the Thomas family compound in the Berkeley hills.

The list of Thomas's work was largely compiled by John Beach and expanded by Jim Stetson. The list is incomplete, lacking the Thomas compound homes on Spruce Street in Berkeley and the home in Diablo. The John Hudson Thomas gallery is a labor of love by Jim Stetson. For more information, visit http://home.earthlink.net/~jimstetson/jht/.

I interviewed Louise Hildebrand Klein in her home, which overlooks Thomas's Hildebrand House.

The Bancroft Library at UC–Berkeley has a collection of architectural drawings. For more information, call 510.642.3781 or visit http://bancroft.berkeley.edu. Thomas Gordon Smith's *John Hudson Thomas and the Progressive Spirit in Architecture* can be found at UC–Berkeley's Environmental Design Library. Charles H. Cheney discussed the work of Plowman and Thomas in "The Art of the Small Home," *House Beautiful* (July 1910). *Bay Area Houses*, edited by Sally Woodbridge (Gibbs Smith, 1988) has essays on Thomas by Beach and David Gebhard.

Frank Wolfe

Much of the biographical material comes from architect and researcher George Espinola, who produced the book *Cottages, Flats, Buildings and Bungalows: 102 Designs by Wolfe & McKenzie* (1907), available from Bay & Valley Publishers, San Jose. For more information, visit www.bayandvalley.com, or contact Espinola at g.espinola@comcast.net.

Birge Clark

Clark's *Unpublished Autobiography of Birge Clark*, in the collection of the Palo Alto Historical Association at the Palo Alto Library, provided biographical information. The association's historian, Steve Staiger, can be reached at the Palo Alto Library.

Biographical information also came from Clark's sons Malcolm and Dean, and from Megan McCaslin, a Palo Alto journalist who interviewed Clark extensively and produced a video about his life. The library provided a list of Clark's buildings, which the architect compiled. Stanford University has a collection of letters between A. B. Clark and Birge Clark and the Hoovers concerning the design of their home at Stanford, along with drawings and plans.

Carr Jones

Ruth Scott, who befriended Jones towards the end of his life and compiled a book about him, *Carr Jones & Doug Allinger: Master Builders Utilizing Recycled Materials*, provided a listing of his buildings and biographical material. The book is available from Scott; call 415.388.5652.

Other biographical information came from Lana Kacsmaryk, his daughter-in-law. Plans for Holly Tree Park, a never-built Jones community in Berkeley, are owned by Scott.

The Berkeley Architectural Heritage Association has lists of Jones's buildings. In their archives is an article by Mara Thiessen Jones, a relative, with information about his life in Yosemite and the lumber camps.

Information about the Rancho Cucamonga home comes from a local application for landmark designation.

Gardner Dailey

The Environmental Design Archives at the University of California (www.ced.berkeley.edu/cedarchive) owns Dailey's papers, mostly drawings, plans and photos, but also newspaper clips, his military records from World War I, letters, and a "History and Background of the Firm" from 1961. The catalog for the Museum of Modern Art's Built in the USA exhibit contains biographical information that came from Dailey himself. Sara Holmes Boutelle told the "Dailey do we not need" story in her "Julia Morgan, Architect," derived from material in the Morgan archive in San Luis Obispo. Joseph Esherick's oral history at the university's Environmental Design Library provided information about Dailey's life and personality. In his oral history, Esherick takes credit for the first drawings for Dailey's Owens House in Sausalito.

Roger Lee

The University of California's short biographical profile of Lee proved useful. His sons Roger Allyn and Roddy Lee and his friend and client Irene Wilkinson provided information about his life and personality. Lee's friend and associate Ted Osmundson rescued Lee's drawings and plans and donated them to the Environmental Design Archives at Berkeley after Lee moved to Hawaii.

Jack Hillmer

Jack Hillmer provided biographical information during a series of interviews. Other material came from written sources, including Alan Hess's "Jack Hillmer's Ludekens House" in the December 1985 *Fine Homebuilding*; "Artistry in Redwood," *Architectural Forum* (September 1960); "Bedroom Pavilion: Excellence of Proportion and Detail," *Western Architect and Engineer* (September 1959); and "Ebony, Granite, Steel and Skill," *Architectural Forum* (April 1951).

Warren Callister

Warren Callister also sat still for extensive interviews. His work has been widely discussed in the architectural press, including: "Warren Callister Is Finding New-Old Ways to Bring Excitement and Warmth Back to the Design Of Homes," *House and Home* (July 1962); "Here's What It Takes To Create a Brand New Market" (about Heritage Village in Connecticut), *House and Home* (April 1967); and a twelve-page spread, plus the cover, on his Duncan Home in *House Beautiful* (February 1962).

Donald Olsen

Donald Olsen discussed his life in a series of interviews. His archives remain in his possession. His Ruth House was profiled in *Architectural Record* (February 1970); in May 1966 *Architectural Record* placed his Cavalier House in Ross among "20 of the finest houses."

Ace Architects

Biographical material comes from an interview with Lucia Howard and David Weingarten. Two books worth reading are *Ten Houses—Ace Architects*, edited by Oscar Riera Ojeda, Rockport Publishers, 2000, and *Bay Area Style: Houses of the San Francisco Bay Region*, by David Weingarten, photos by Alan Weintraub. This is Weingarten's take on the Bay Region style.

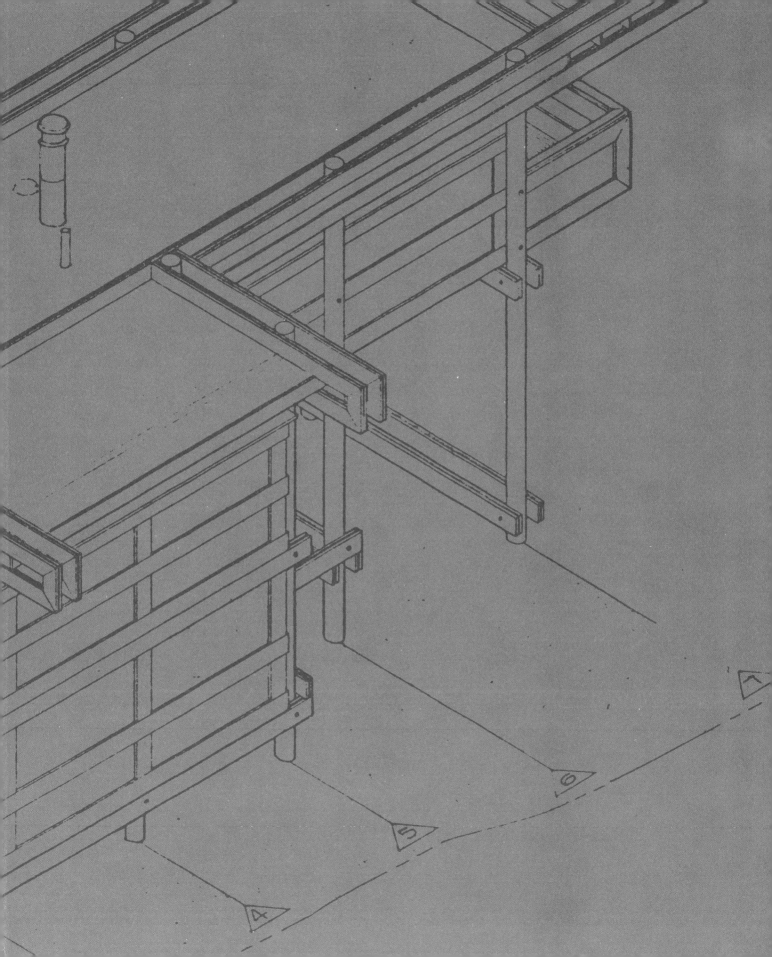